Conversations with an Immortal

Don Durrett

Copyright © 2010 by Donald David Durrett
All rights reserved.

(Fourth Edition October 2023)

Library of Congress Control Number: 2010942784

No part of this book may be reproduced in any form or by any electronic or mechanical means including information storage and retrieval systems, without permission in writing from the author.

ISBN: 978-1-4276-5063-4

www.dondurrett.com

Books by Don Durrett

A Stranger From the Past

Spirit Club

New Thinking for the New Age

Finding Your Soul

Last of the Gnostics

The Gathering

Ascension Training

Team Creator

The Way

The Path Forward

Get Healthy / Stay Healthy

America's Political Cold War

Post America: A New Constitution

The Demise of America

Cake and eat it, that's what you want. But that slice is going to kill you and it's time you found out.
—World Party

In the end, only kindness matters.
—Jewel

Do unto others as you would have them do unto you.
—The Golden Rule

Reader's Review

We learn what the future has in store for us ... and that exhilarating insight is the true value of *Conversations With an Immortal*. You may agree or disagree with author Don Durrett's predictions, but never with his superb writing style and brilliant philosophy.

– *Richard Fuller*, Metaphysical Reviews

Introduction

We are quickly approaching an epical period for humanity. Our current civilization is about to evolve into something much better than exists today. Soon, a tumultuous transition period will begin, leading to a new civilization based on love and humanity.

I have been writing books about this transition since 1991, when I wrote *A Stranger From the Past*. Now, in the new millennium, we are getting close. I will be surprised if the next few years do not bring revolutionary changes for civilization.

What has occurred this century, beginning with 9/11 (September 11, 2001), then the GFC (Great Financial Crisis) in 2008, the Presidency of Donald Trump in 2016, followed by the COVID crisis in 2020, were all precursors of what is in store for America and the world. The culmination of these events will change our way of life and expectations of the future.

I write about metaphysical spirituality. In particular, I write about the spirituality of the future. I write about what people will believe *after* the transition (or what is called the Great Shift in the newage community). I will give you a hint: People will not believe what they do today. These are new beliefs for a *New Age*, or a new civilization, whichever term you prefer.

The purpose of my writing is to share what is coming and inspire people to contemplate spirituality from a metaphysical perspective. You may not believe me, but soon spiritual beliefs will be dominated by metaphysical concepts, such as there is only one consciousness of which we all share.

I do not profess to be enlightened or to know the ultimate truth. If you disagree with some of my ideas, that's fine. In fact, I don't want you to accept everything in this book, because we each need to discover the truth for ourselves. In fact, we each need to hold our *own* individual truth. No two people can hold the same truth and same beliefs.

This book is about the coming transition, which will be a period of dramatic societal change that will lead to a new civilization. It includes scenarios that can occur and spiritual beliefs that will likely become widely accepted. It is written in the present tense, with an eye towards the near future. It is a wake-up call for what is quickly approaching.

I originally wrote this book in 1994, updating it in 2006, 2013, and now 2023. It is amazing how much has changed in the last thirty years and that what I wrote in 1994 has nearly come to pass. The changes are clearly upon us and have become apparent to most. Although what I describe might be a bit extreme, what I see coming will be nothing short of traumatic and transformational for society and for individuals. Our beliefs and way of life will literally transform. This book will give you a glimpse of that transformation.

Donald David Durrett
October, 2023

Contents

Reader's Review vi

Introduction vii

Chapter One
Hopi Reservation Part 1 1

Chapter Two
Hopi Reservation Part 2 15

Chapter Three
Los Angeles Lecture 37

Chapter Four
Trip to San Francisco 69

Chapter Five
San Francisco Lecture 103

Chapter Six
Trip to Seattle 125

Chapter Seven
Seattle Lecture 139

Endnotes 164

Conversations with an Immortal

Chapter One

Hopi Reservation Part 1

I drove from Los Angeles to the Four Corners region (the intersection of Arizona, Utah, Colorado, and New Mexico) to meet a man I knew only by reputation. Peter Vaughn was living in the northeast corner of Arizona on the Hopi Reservation. He was Caucasian, yet was teaching the Hopi about spirituality. This intrigued me. He had to be extremely spiritual.

I was hoping I could convince him to join me on my upcoming lecture tour. He had been recommended by a friend of mine. I thought about writing a letter or phoning him, but I decided that a face-to-face meeting would be the right approach.

I drove to Durango, Colorado, where I found a hotel room. The next morning, I drove to the Hopi Reservation and tried to find Peter. After I parked my car and asked a few people where I could find him, I was told by a middle-aged Hopi man who seemed to be in charge that Peter wasn't available. I had been told by a psychic friend before I left Los Angeles that this might be difficult, and to be patient. So, I had anticipated returning to the reservation for several days.

On days two and three, the same thing happened.

On the fourth day, the Hopi who had been my nemesis, finally met me with a smile and a warm greeting. "He will see you now."

I had expected to be turned away again because, for the past three days, there had been no indication I would get to speak with him. Today, however, I was received in a much different manner and ushered inside Peter's pueblo.

My psychic friend had told me that Peter would know me and that we would have a long conversation, but that the outcome of the meeting was unknown. There was a possibility of success, but also a possibility of failure. I knew that I had a chance, and that was why I was here.

I had not seen a picture of Peter and didn't know what to expect. I was greatly surprised when I saw him. He was younger than me. I had expected an older man, perhaps even elderly, not an adult in the prime of his life.

We shook hands and smiled at each other without either of us saying a word. Immediately, I could sense that we had a lot in common. He was approximately thirty-five years of age, tall and thin, with long, dark brown hair and sharp, handsome features.

"My name is John Randall," I said to him in my usual serious tone. "A friend of mine suggested that I should meet you, and that we might be able to help each other."

He motioned for me to sit. "Have a seat, and we can talk."

I sat, and he found a chair across from me. We were alone in what looked to be a study room of some kind. The simple, single-room pueblo was at least fifty years old, probably much older. It wasn't clean or nice, but simply functional. It was made of stone and clay mortar, with whitewashed, plaster-coated walls. An old hand-loomed carpet covered most of the floor. A beautiful Native American painting hung on one of the walls. It seemed out of place, but then, so was Peter. We both sat in worn leather chairs that were functional but had seen their better days. There was also a

Chapter One - Hopi Reservation Part 1

tattered leather sofa and a bookshelf with hundreds of books. In front of the sofa, a book lay open on a coffee table.

"You're an admired and respected figure in the New Age community," I said. "Recently, I talked to several people who've heard about you. It's acknowledged that you are an excellent spiritual teacher."

Peter raised his eyebrows. "Well, that is quite a compliment. Hmm. I wonder how the word spread. I have taught here on the reservation since 1998, when I arrived in America from Europe. Only a handful of white people have been to my lectures."

I looked at Peter closely. There was something unusual about him. I realized that it was his skin. I didn't want to pry, but I felt the urge. "Were you born on this planet, or is there something *unusual* about you?"

"Hmm. Can you keep a secret?" He said it with an intensity that was surprising in its magnitude.

I hesitated to reply, finally sputtering, "Yes," but unsure if I was telling the truth.

"I was born in Egypt in approximately 1000 B.C.," Peter said. "I learned how to stop the aging process. In a way, I am immortal, although I could allow myself to age if I so desired."

I was shocked and stared at him in astonishment and disbelief.

"Why did you tell me something so personal?" I asked, amazed.

Peter smiled back at me. "Two reasons. First, I don't think you will go around telling all of your friends that you met an immortal. Second, I plan on leaving the planet soon. Once the vibration of the planet rises high enough, I plan on ascending to the New Earth in the fifth dimension."

I smiled. "I'll bet you will. I've always believed that immortals existed. I just never expected to meet one."

Peter continued smiling. "John, I have a good feeling we are going to be friends. I am sorry you had to wait so long to see me. In fact, I did not know you were here until yesterday. The Hopi protect me and honor my privacy.

"Your reputation, John, is the only reason I was even told that you were trying to see me. Someone recognized you yesterday and mentioned you to me. Usually, they will not allow visitors.

"When I was told you were here, I looked up your Akashic record. It seems we have a lot in common. We are both old soul priests, although I am sixth level to your fifth. In this lifetime, we both chose to help during the transition, although I decided to have three thousand years of preparation," Peter smiled.

I grinned at his attempt at humor. "How much do you know about the future?" I asked. I was completely at ease in his presence and was enjoying the conversation.

"What you know … and a little more. I have a few more sources than you. Basically, we both know that the transition is almost upon us and that it will be traumatic, leading to a new civilization."

"You're a sixth-level old soul priest?" I asked rhetorically. "In your three thousand years, you must have spent hundreds of years becoming spiritually aware. You must be one of the most aware people on the planet."

Peter nodded. "Yes, that is true. During my three thousand years, I have spent most of my life as a student or a teacher of spirituality. Like yourself, I am now exposing others to the spiritual knowledge I have learned."

"Why here, on the Hopi Reservation?" I asked. "Why not spread the word to the general public?"

Chapter One – Hopi Reservation Part 1

"I am waiting," Peter replied, "and this is where I chose to wait. It is too early to go public. You and I both are waiting for the transition to begin and as you know, very few people care about what we have to say at this time. The spiritual philosophy we teach is simply too advanced for most of society. Few are ready to acknowledge that they are this only one consciousness, which we all share."

"May I ask you some questions?"

Peter crossed his legs and changed his sitting position. "Sure, go ahead."

"Define the concept of oneness."

Peter looked confused. "Why? You already understand it."

"Humor me," I said. "I want to know how well *you* understand it."

Peter laughed. "Oneness is the basic fact that nothing is separate from the Creator's consciousness. If you want to give this consciousness a name, let us call it God. So, God is everything: all-that-is.

"Because God is all-that-is and God is perfection, *everything* is perfection, and *everything* is divinely ordered. Thus, there is no right or wrong. There is only perfection. In other words, all experiences are valid. It is just as valid for someone to experience the negative as the positive. It is just as valid for someone to experience murder as to experience love. In both cases, it is God experiencing these events, not someone separate from God.

"We are eternal because we are God. There is no God or Creator separate from us. We are as much a part of God as is any other fragment of consciousness that comprises God. There is no separation because *everything* comprises the whole. In other words, God is the whole. Conversely, for God to materialize as a being, we were created. For this reason,

God cannot judge us, because we are God. God cannot save us or give us eternal life, because we already *are* God."

Peter looked deeply into my eyes. "Currently, the world is based on the concept that we are separate from God, but separation is a lie, and thus, the world is currently built on top of lies. This belief in separation has created the duality upon which this planet's civilization is based: right and wrong, good and evil. It's all lies. There is no duality.

"The world's acceptance of this duality has actually created the negative experiences that pervade this planet. In fact, once the truth is known, the negativity will cease. Why? Because the truth is that we are God, and our core is love. Love will manifest once the truth is known.

"Once we become aware of the divinity in all things and all people, love will flourish. It is a matter of awareness of the concept of oneness. For, we cannot judge others once we become aware that they are divine; we cannot manipulate them; we cannot kill them; we cannot even damage the environment. Love is the automatic outcome of the awareness of our oneness. This new awareness is transformational.

"My motto is the following: If I want to be happy, I love. I love myself, and I love others. Not just those I want to love, but everyone and everything. Also, I do not have expectations or try to control the outcomes in my life. I am only grateful, grateful for the opportunity to experience who I am: God. So, all we get are opportunities and blessings. That's it. Everything else is a lie."

I laughed. "Are you sure you haven't been reading my books?"

Peter laughed back. "I can probably guess what you have written: intense spiritual material that few understand.

Chapter One - Hopi Reservation Part 1

You are probably frustrated by this. However, you persevere, waiting for the transition to begin."

I nodded. "So, is Nostradamus correct? Will the foundation for the next civilization be based on the New Age movement in America? And is that why you came here?"

"To answer your last question, yes, this is where the action will be. America, and the western United States, is where the spiritual foundation will be laid. Is Nostradamus correct? Why would he not be? He saw it with his own eyes. He was the greatest psychic who ever lived. I remember walking into his house in 1555 after he had published his first quatrains. At first, he was suspicious of me, until he recognized my ancient age. He thought it was fascinating that I would someday see his visions come to pass. I stayed for several weeks. When I finally left, I was probably one of his best friends. He was a great man, and I miss him."

I shook my head in awe. "How many other incredible experiences have you had? And what inspired you to visit Nostradamus?"

"I have spent most of my life in Europe because that is where the action used to be. After Nostradamus published his quatrains, he became widely known. He was a celebrity of sorts. Yes, I have had a few experiences with historical figures. I have lived through history."

"You said that you lived in Europe. What can you tell me about the Order of Scion and the Knights Templar?"

"Why?" Peter asked. "What do *you* know about them?"

"I've read about them in a couple of books, but I wish I knew more. I know that the Order of Scion supposedly still exists and is quite powerful. That it is composed of prominent citizens, mainly European. That it is secretive. The members are initiated with certain doctrines and beliefs about Mary Magdalene and Jesus' descendants. The leader is called the Grand Master and is said to be related by blood to Jesus' progeny."

I continued with what I knew about the Scion. "The Order is said to harbor a desire to create a monarchy over the whole of Europe, with the Grand Master as king. It is widely believed that the Order is constantly conniving and planning to achieve this goal, and that their underlying belief that Jesus' progeny are sacred, has kept the organization together.

"The Knights Templar are historical fact," I added. "They came into existence shortly after the First Crusade, in 1099, and their original members came from southern France. Many believe that the Knights Templar were created by Scion as a foothold to power. The Knights Templar did, indeed, become powerful. They were the original bankers of Europe and became incredibly wealthy. Eventually, on Friday, October 13, 1307, the Knights were rounded up and arrested over the whole of Europe by order of the King of France, who wanted their money. Up until then, the Knights had been almost as powerful as the Catholic Church. These wealthy and secretive Knights were called 'warrior monks,' and were among the first Christian monks."

I paused, collecting my thoughts. "A Knight was initiated into the Order for life. He gave up all of his possessions to the group, and he lived with the Knights in secret. There are many fascinating things about the Knights that history has never revealed. What happened to their treasure? What did they believe? We know that the Catholic Church reviled them and put up with them only because of their wealth and power. One of their beliefs was that they did not consider Jesus different from themselves. They were Gnostics and considered him their equal, which was anathema to Catholicism.

Chapter One - Hopi Reservation Part 1

"The Knights believed that faith is a personal experience, not something provided by God's surrogates, such as Catholic priests. And they revered Mary Magdalene. Many think this was because she came to southern France with a child named Sarah, who was supposedly fathered by Jesus. Scion believes the progeny of Sarah are the descendants of Jesus. There are historical records of Mary Magdalene and Sarah living in southern France. The Troubadours, and to this day the Gypsies, sing songs to a lady named Sarah."

I stopped and waited for Peter's reply. I felt he knew a lot more than I did about these mysterious groups, and I wanted to learn more.

"You know your history well, John. Yes, it was Scion who created the Knights. In the late eleventh century, after the Crusades brought Palestine back into the hands of the Christians, Scion wanted to create a power base in Israel. They used the Knights as an army to protect their interests. A member of Scion, Godfroi de Baudouin, was put in charge of Palestine. He was French, and his title was King of Jerusalem. This very interesting history is largely ignored today. I suppose it is because the Moors, the Arabs, took back control of Palestine a few decades later.

"However, it was Europe that was the center of Scion's interest. During the early twelfth century, the Knights accumulated land and money, and, as you said, John, they became as powerful as the Catholic Church."

Peter paused for a moment and looked at me. "*I* was a Templar Knight. In fact, I was in France on October 13, 1307, which was the worst day of my long life. Hundreds of my friends were arrested, tortured, and killed. I escaped on foot to Spain.

"As you know, the Knights were destroyed by the Catholic Church with the help of the French monarchy.

The King of France gave the order, but he was the Church's proxy. I have not had much respect for the Church since that day. It is one of my most sorrowful memories. I still grieve today."

Peter sat comfortably, with his legs crossed, and continued in an effortless manner, yet an underlying passion and intensity was evident. "The Order was a spiritual brotherhood, and the Knights were amazing. There has been no one like them since. They were initiates and truly spiritual men. The sense of brotherhood among them has not been equaled in history. Their closeness was incredible. When the Inquisition attempted to torture the Knights, none of them talked. Many of my friends were tortured to death without saying a word. They did not reveal their secrets.

"The Church did not want to hear the truth, that everyone was Jesus' equal, that Jesus was God, and so were they. How could the Knights tell their inquisitors the truth? It would have brought only more torture and the label of 'heresy.' The Church wanted to know their secrets, yet was not prepared to accept them.

"I learned a lot as a Knight Templar. Courage, integrity, spiritual awareness, brotherhood. I have been waiting for the end of the current civilization, so that I can see these values manifest again. Soon, there will be groups of people forming spiritual communities. People again will be initiates and expected to uphold the values of their communities.

"The Knights Templar," Peter continued, with even more passion, "were not only the proxies of the Order of Scion. They also were the guardians of truth. That is how they got their name: Knights Templar. They were guardians of the temple. The temple represents spirituality and spiritual knowledge. The temple is where the truth resides.

Chapter One - Hopi Reservation Part 1

"The Knights Templar were warrior-monks who guarded the spiritual knowledge that the Church was trying to repress. When they were broken up in 1307, the Gnostic branch of Christianity was severed. From then until the nineteenth century, Gnostic knowledge was repressed and largely lost. In the nineteenth century, occultism became popular, and Gnostic knowledge began to be disseminated again.

"Today, the New Age movement has blossomed and is positioned to replace the Catholic Church and all of the other Christian denominations that dominate Western spirituality. The concepts that I studied with the Knights are once again flourishing. It has been a long wait."

Peter stretched his arms and found a more comfortable position in his chair. "For me, the Renaissance never occurred. From my perspective, the Dark Ages began in the fourteenth century, when the Knights were killed, and they have continued to this day. From the time I was born in Egypt, until the early fourteenth century, I was able to discuss Gnostic ideas with educated people. What is not understood today is that the Gnostics had a profound effect on spiritual issues until the fourteenth century. So much was lost and is not recognized by today's historians.

"I find it fascinating how naïve people are today regarding spirituality. The Christian Church, along with the other religious doctrines on this planet, has left the vast majority of people clueless regarding spiritual truth. Everyone is in a fog, unaware of even the simplest truths. Yes, the New Age movement is expanding, but the majority of people are still oblivious to spirituality and the truth.

"We are headed toward a time of dramatic change, yet the vast majority of people are clueless as to *why* this is happening. It is incredible. So few people know that they are

God and that we share the same consciousness. So few know that everything is already perfect and divinely ordered. We are destroying the planet and creating untold trauma simply because we are oblivious to our true identity. However, that spiritual ignorance is shortly coming to an end.

"When the transition begins," Peter continued, "the majority of Americans are going to be anxious. They will be afraid and disillusioned. I do not know exactly how it will transpire, but I do know that very few are prepared. I suppose that is why we are both here, to somehow help during this transition."

"How will we know when the transition has begun?" I asked.

"When people lose faith in the future of America," Peter said solemnly. "When people begin talking about the recent past in nostalgic terms. When people acknowledge that the future is not going to look anything like the past, then society will begin changing rapidly.

"An analogy can be made to the Roman Empire," he continued. "Once the Empire was near the end, there was a noticeable recognition that the Empire was doomed. That is what I am waiting for: a recognition that our current way of life is no longer possible and for behaviors to begin to change. This time, however, the change is going to be spiritual in nature. It is going to be the biggest spiritual revolution this planet has ever seen, and we both have a front row seat."

Peter smiled and looked at me with his penetrating eyes. "Now, John, what brought you here today?"

I smiled. "Well, before we change the subject, I do have a few more questions about Scion and the Knights Templar, but I can save them for later."

Peter nodded, acknowledging that we would talk more later about his past.

Chapter One - Hopi Reservation Part 1

"I came to find out if you will join me on a lecture tour. My lectures could use a spark, and I'm looking for another speaker. I have a three-city tour planned: Los Angeles, San Francisco, and Seattle. You were recommended, and now that we have met, I think destiny has played a part in bringing us together."

"Hmm," Peter murmured, then contemplated for several seconds. "I suppose it is time. I cannot hide in a closet and help humanity at the same time."

I smiled. "It's a short tour, and the first lecture is in two weeks. I'm scheduled to speak alone, but no one will care if you do it with me. The lectures are scheduled for two hours. I figure we can each speak for about thirty minutes, and then answer questions."

Peter nodded. "All expenses will be paid in advance?"

"Yes, and you will get paid as well. Five thousand dollars, which is half of the contract."

"And I can talk about whatever I want?"

I nodded. "Of course. The subject is up to you."

"I think I am going to enjoy this adventure. Will it be only the two of us?"

"Yes. Just you and me. Do you have any other questions?"

"John, you appear to have everything planned. Is there anything I need to do, such as get a ride to Los Angeles, or anything else?"

I shook my head. "I'll pick you up here and bring you back after the tour is over. As long as you don't mind long car rides or staying in hotels, everything has been taken into consideration."

Peter nodded. "Then it will be the two of us driving this entire trip?"

"Yes. We'll drive from here to Los Angeles for the first lecture, then on to San Francisco, and last to Seattle. We might visit a few of my friends on the way. Is that okay with you?"

Peter smiled. "Sounds like a fun road trip. Now, what were those other questions?"

Chapter Two

Hopi Reservation Part 2

I smiled at this wise, peaceful, and kind man. I considered myself very fortunate to have met Peter. I didn't have the slightest worry that the trip would be anything but enjoyable.

"Does Scion still exist?"

Peter shook his head. "No, they dispersed after the Templars were arrested. Perhaps there is a group who claims to be Scion, but they are playing a fool's charade."

"Was Sarah the daughter of Jesus and Mary Magdalene?"

"Yes, and they were married. My understanding is that Mary was pregnant when Jesus died on the cross. Mary Magdalene brought Sarah to southern France, and Sarah's children became the descendants of the Merovingian kings, the first Christian kings of France.

"Mary Magdalene was the daughter of Joseph of Arimathea, who was the older stepbrother of Mother Mary. Jesus and Mary Magdalene were actually first cousins. One important piece of history that has been lost is that Mary Magdalene and Sarah were the progenitors that led to the Cathars in southern France. This majestic Gnostic group was murdered by the Catholic Church during the Albigensian Crusade in the thirteenth century."

He stopped, and I wondered if he was right.

"What happened to the Templars' treasure?" I asked.

"It was taken to Scotland and then buried on Oak Island, near Nova Scotia. People have been trying to find it for centuries without success."

"How many years were you a Knight Templar?" I asked, "Did you spend time in Jerusalem?"

"Yes, I was in Jerusalem during the early twelfth century. I wore a white robe with a large red cross emblem stitched on the front, which was a Gnostic cross that originated in southern France. I was part of the group that protected Jerusalem after the First Crusade. It was a thrilling time. There were about a thousand Knights in Jerusalem. We lived in the temple at night and protected the roads during the day.

"That was when the Knights came into existence. We were called the Knights Templar because we lived in the temple. We were more knights than monks in the beginning. There was no time for spiritual work because we were too busy guarding the city. However, the foundation was laid for our group to become monks. After we were overrun by the Moors, we went back to Europe and did just that. From then on, the warrior aspect of the organization was secondary, and we were monks first and foremost."

Peter continued. "I was a Knight during the entire period of the Knights Templar, for over 200 years. How did I do it? I moved around. It was actually quite easy. You have to remember that life spans were much shorter then. So, when I moved back to an area, no one recognized me. I just started a new life in a new region or a new country."

"Tell me about the spiritual work you did with the Knights," I asked.

"Well, we had some very good ancient texts: Plato, Socrates, Philo, Valentinius. Many of these came from

Chapter Two - Hopi Reservation Part 2

Alexandria and were copies of ancient Atlantean documents. The Atlanteans were very advanced spiritually. They knew a lot about spiritual truth. The Knights studied documents that do not exist today. How the documents came to us, I do not know. I suppose the Knights acquired them because of the power and wealth we amassed. We had some very influential members. I guess they wanted to share their secrets with fellow comrades."

Peter got up and looked out the only window in the room. "It is sad that the documents did not survive. When the Knights were rounded up and arrested, all of their documents were destroyed. There might be a text or two around today, but I would be surprised to see anything published."

Peter noticed my anxiousness to hear more about the spirituality of the Atlanteans and what he had studied as a Knight. He smiled. "Okay, John, I will tell you more. I can see that you want to hear as much as possible.

"We studied texts that focused on the inherent divinity of all things: that nothing is separate from God; that, in essence, everything is God. Not only is everything God, but everything is connected and interacting. Everything is dependent on the interaction with its environment. In other words, nothing exists in a vacuum.

"People think they are separate from Source and separate from each other, but that's not true. We all share the same consciousness of the Creator. Everything does.

"The extent of one's impact on its surrounding environment is much more prevalent than is commonly understood. For instance, we act and react based on the input of our surrounding environment. Not a single experience occurs without the surrounding environment dictating the experience. We think we have free will, but that is an illusion. Our surrounding environment has a much more profound effect because we are all connected."

Peter came back and sat in his chair. "Let me try to explain the significance of the environment. We, the mass consciousness or collective whole, believe that air has no substance, that air has no impact on our lives other than for breathing. What if I were to tell you that air is the conduit of energy and is as vibrant and alive as organic life?

"Right now, as we speak, energy is flowing back and forth between us through the air. This energy is affecting both of us in a substantial manner. And not only are we interacting with our own energy, but also the energy of people on this reservation and the energy from people all over the world. Energy from the environment bombards us and affects us. We cannot escape its grip."

Peter was animated and spoke passionately. "Energy is how God communicates. In many respects, God is energy. God can know what everything is doing by listening to the energy. Likewise, God can influence events by influencing the energy. Remember, God is not a being. God is everything. However, because God is everything, God can influence events. Just as we can bend a finger, God can influence us to bend a finger. Think of God as having the ability to influence outcomes. God listens to the energy and feels the energy, then responds.

"God's impact in our lives cannot be underestimated. We are deluding ourselves when we think we live in a vacuum, making our own decisions, and creating our own lives. God is as involved in our decision-making as we are, perhaps even more. As I said earlier, the environment, which is God, is much more prevalent in our lives than we realize.

"Scientists have learned through experiments that atoms have a way of communicating no matter the distance. Not

Chapter Two - Hopi Reservation Part 2

only that, but the location of an atom can be determined only through the reference of the observer, which makes reality subjective. In other words, where I see an atom and where you see the same atom, are not always in the same location. Scientists have been puzzled by these observations and have made very little progress in understanding the results of their experiments. However, this will change soon.

"Scientists will now begin to make progress on understanding that atoms are conscious and intelligent, although it will take several decades for scientists to fully understand the results of their experiments. However, it won't be long now before scientists are able to determine that all things are related consciously. After this truth has been disseminated, the world will be a completely new place. The belief in separation will be a thing of the past, much like the world being flat."

I slowly shook my head in amazement, listening to his knowledge, as Peter continued on.

"Because we are God, there is really very little to achieve, because there is nothing that God needs to do. We can play our little games, such as who has the most money or who is the smartest, but it is all a charade. We each get to play all of the roles. We get to be king, queen, artist, musician, pauper, magnate, and everything in between. In the end, it is just a way for God to evolve. Stated another way, life is God having fun, or perhaps avoiding boredom. Take your pick. Or, stated another way, the meaning of life is life itself. In other words, life is the meaning."

Peter gestured with his hands facing up. "Currently, this planet is spiritually ignorant. It is like the movie, *The Matrix*, where no one realizes that they are in a computer simulation. Today, nearly everyone in America believes this is their first lifetime. People believe they are separate from God and separate from each other. This duality has created the negative experiences that are so prevalent today. God created this ignorance specifically to experience the negative. For, without amnesia of our true identity, negative experiences would be difficult to create. With amnesia, experiences become unbounded."

I considered asking a question, but I didn't want to stop the beautiful words that I was hearing. It was like a symphony or a play. It was better just to sit back and listen.

"Would people consume drugs, commit crimes, or judge others in harsh terms, if they knew that everyone is God? No way. It would not happen. That is why the spiritual ignorance is so widespread. If people are going to experience negative emotions, they have to be ignorant of their true identity.

"This is the knowledge I learned from the Atlantean texts that I read as a Knight Templar. Over the many years since, I have found enough correlating data to support these ideas. In fact, all of the channeled material that began in the 1960s with Jane Roberts confirmed what I learned as a Knight.

"People today are relearning the very things I learned eight hundred years ago. That is why the transition will be successful. Thousands of people are ready to expose others to what they know. When the time is right, the Internet will spread the truth like a contagious virus.

"Considering the degree of change that is going take place within the span of one generation, that is the only way it can happen. And it will. Within one generation, the current generation, society will transform itself from being based on power to being based on love. This will occur because the majority will know the truth of their identity.

Chapter Two – Hopi Reservation Part 2

"While the transition will begin with this generation, it will actually require four generations to fully transform. We will put it in motion, but to completely purge old beliefs cannot be done quickly. There will be many who resist change, but their resistance will be futile. The truth is destined to be the foundation of the next civilization. All lies will eventually be purged.

"How is this possible? The answer is one word: vibration. Consciousness is energy, and energy vibrates. All consciousness has been steadily increasing in vibration. For instance, our bodies vibrate between 80,000 to 100,000 cycles per second. As we vibrate faster, we become more spiritual and more aware of who we are. This increase in vibration does not decrease; it only increases. So, as our bodies, souls, and the mass consciousness increase in vibration, it becomes more difficult for lies to exist. Thus, they are steadily purged, leaving only the truth. This is God's grand plan.

"The Atlanteans knew the truth. They had very little crime or poverty. They lived in harmony for thousands of years. There was widespread knowledge of the truth. The amount of love that flourished in their civilization was spectacular. They loved each other so much that people were treated fairly. If you wanted to do something in Atlantis, you either were given the opportunity or presented with an alternative of your liking.

"With love came compassion, understanding, and empathy. It is amazing how little love flows today between strangers, and yet we think we are civilized."

Peter raised his eyebrows and then continued on with his passionate intensity. "This planet is in the dark ages, and the vast majority of the population has no idea of the true reality that exists. Instead, there is prevalent ignorance. I shake my head in wonder. As a civilization, there have been few spiritual advances on this planet in the last ten thousand years. In fact, as a civilization, we have regressed spiritually, although during the last thirty years, things have begun to change.

"Spiritual avatars such as Jesus and Buddha helped many to advance spiritually. I consider Jesus' teachings to be the foundation of my spirituality. However, as a civilization, we have neglected his teachings and, in fact, have institutionalized the opposite. Jesus preached humanity, equality, and love for our fellow human beings. The Scandinavian countries have done a reasonable job with these values, but the rest of the world has failed miserably.

"The New Age movement has begun to have a positive impact on this civilization, although the people who resonate as New Agers have little societal power, and the New Age movement itself is largely a well-kept secret. This is rapidly changing as people like Wayne Dyer, Deepak Chopra, and Eckhart Tolle are seen by millions on television.

"Most New Agers do not tell their friends or families about their beliefs and practices. In many respects, New Agers have not come out of the closet, to borrow a phrase from the gay movement. They are not the movers and shakers of society. Most people think of New Agers as strange, mainly because their beliefs do not match their own. To say that the New Age movement has not yet reached mainstream is an accurate assessment. New Agers are in the minority, and the movement is largely stigmatized.

"This group, however, is gaining momentum. Notice the increased popularity of shows on television regarding paranormal, extraterrestrial, and esoteric themes. All of these TV shows put a strain on the existing beliefs that we are alone in the universe and that our spiritual foundations are sound.

Chapter Two - Hopi Reservation Part 2

"It is the New Ager who is comfortable talking about UFOs, paranormal subjects, and Gnostic philosophy. And these subjects are having more and more impact on society. People are becoming comfortable with these ideas and beliefs. Trust me when I say that extraterrestrials will land soon. This event will have an enormous impact. New Agers will welcome this validation with fervor. Those who wish to hold onto the beliefs of the past will be in for a fight, not with weapons, but ideas. The New Agers will rise as a group. They will make a compelling argument for the significance of this landing event. Their voice will be heard, and nothing will be the same again."

Peter paused. "Sorry, I kind of lost track of what I was talking about. Oh, yes, the Atlanteans. Their grasp of truth created a virtual paradise for a long period. I am optimistic that this planet will return to that kind of spiritual paradise. All it takes is awareness, and the growing New Age movement is setting the foundation for such a spiritual leap forward. More and more people are learning the truth of their identity. It is a very subtle revolution, but a revolution nonetheless. It is happening as we speak."

Peter paused again. "Do you have any questions?"

I smiled. "You are incredibly knowledgeable. I'm glad our lectures will be recorded so that more people can hear your words. Yes, I have a question. If the Atlanteans did not believe in good and evil, what were their moral codes?"

Peter adjusted his position to get more comfortable. "Good question. They believed in their own divinity, and they did not believe in sin. Their morality was based on honor. People were expected to behave in certain ways based on societal norms. If the norms were ignored, pressure was applied in various ways. People could be asked to leave the community. Jails did not exist, so banishment was the only real form of punishment."

"What happened to Atlantis?"

"No one knows definitively, but there are many theories. The most accepted is that they destroyed themselves by misusing crystal technology. What probably happened is that Atlantis existed for thousands of years in relative harmony. Then, toward the end, the people in power coveted more power. Instead of a civilization based on love, power became the determinant of the culture. It did not take long for those in power to be consumed with maintaining power. Once that occurred, their civilization began to languish. Then, it was only a matter of time before their eventual demise.

"How the continent sunk is irrelevant," Peter continued. "Why the continent sunk yields wisdom. The reason was disharmony. The planet Earth, along with its plant life, animals, and people, all live as one. When this harmony is disrupted, there are ramifications. That is the lesson people come to experience, one lifetime after another, that God is perfect harmony. People learn this law through many incarnations.

"When we create disharmony with our free choice, it is only a matter of time before God intervenes. Intervention also occurs when there is harmony. God is always intervening. God does not just appear when there is a problem. Life is God in action. Intervention can be subtle, or it can be dramatic…"

"So," I interrupted, "you are trying to tell me that God is intervening today? God has a plan to transform our culture from one based on power to one based on love?"

Peter nodded. "Yes. I call it God's grand plan to restore harmony by exposing the truth. Intervention is what this transition is all about. Is it not interesting that, just like Rome,

Chapter Two - Hopi Reservation Part 2

the people in power today are corrupt and only interested in maintaining the status quo? The ruling class, and I'm not talking about politicians, but those who really wield power, think their behavior is appropriate. However, they should feel guilty about manipulating the economic system to their advantage. Instead, they are concerned about making more money. All this does is to create more disharmony, with more wealth accumulating in the hands of the few.

"In many ways, today is similar to the end of Rome. The American empire is losing its global influence; we are spending large amounts of money on wars we cannot afford; our culture has become obsessed with entertainment as an escape; our debts are mounting, and our money is depreciating; and corruption is rampant.

"Of course, there are many differences. The most significant is that today, the potential exists for a spiritual transformation. Not only does the potential exist, but the potential will manifest…"

"But how," I interrupted, "can you be so sure?"

"I *ch*. A transformation is coming very soon. What is unknown is exactly how the transformation will occur. It will be, however, chaotic. Economic implosion, political incompetence, and societal decay, all lead to transformation. One, two, three. The only question is, 'How chaotic?' Natural disasters will play a part. Expect an unusual number of floods, hurricanes, earthquakes, and volcanoes. This scenario will inevitably lead to social chaos and will be the signal that the transition has begun."

Peter raised his eyebrows. "How many prophets do we need? Nostradamus, St. Malachi, Edgar Cayce, the Hopi, the Mayans, Ruth Montgomery, Lee Carroll, Dolores Cannon. Could they all be wrong? I suppose it is possible, but it is not what I expect."

I nodded. "Yes, I agree. Everything points to a transformation into a new civilization. Some type of great shift."

"The evidence is overwhelming," Peter continued. "One of the ancient texts that I read while I was a Knight came from the Essenes. It was likely Atlantean and copied by the Essenes. This document foretold the era of Jesus. It was written before he was born. It predicted his life and the era he would spawn. It was a marvelous text that was insightful and highly accurate. What is interesting about this document is that it not only predicted Jesus' era, but also the era's demise. The year given for the end of the Jesus era was 2012. I think that is when the transition began.

"Did you know that the Mayan calendar suddenly stops on the twenty-first of December, 2012? Very interesting, would you not say? What did the Mayans and Essenes have in common that they could predict events thousands of years into the future? Also, what about all of the people who have reiterated this prediction over the years? Something is going to happen, and soon."

"I agree," I said. "I'm expecting it, too."

"Have you heard of the prophecy of the Hopi?" Peter asked, still animated after talking for nearly an hour. "It is astonishingly accurate. Ask any Hopi who has knowledge of the prophecy, and he or she will tell you that the fourth world, the current civilization, is about to come to an end, and that the Hopi will have their land and culture back during the fifth world, after the transition. The Hale-Bopp comet that appeared in the sky in March 1997 is connected to the Hopi prophecy."

Peter looked into my eyes. "You have heard of the Hale-Bopp comet, John?"

Chapter Two – Hopi Reservation Part 2

I nodded. "Yes, it was an amazing sight. I drove up to the mountains to see it clearly. It was an incredibly large comet that lit up the sky."

"The prophecy states that a blue star will appear as a sign of the imminent demise of the fourth world," Peter continued. "Hale-Bopp is the blue star. It had a blue hue and was the most brilliant comet to appear in recent years.

"Indeed, the blue star signified the imminent start of the transition. I have been waiting for centuries for this moment. It is difficult for me not to get excited. I have not been this excited since the eleventh century, when I studied with the Knights." Peter smiled.

"I'm excited, as well," I said. "I've been waiting since 1989. That's when I learned about the future. I've been waiting patiently, just like you." I grinned. "And, like you, I understand the magnitude of the coming transition. We're going to experience a magnitude of change that is rare in the cosmos. This kind of transformation, from spiritual ignorance to spiritual awareness in less than one generation, is very rare. Those who get to experience it are very fortunate. I, like yourself, realize the magnitude of what is about to occur."

At that moment, I realized that I could ask Peter any question and he would try to answer. He was an open book, and love shone brilliantly from him. "Have you ever met another immortal?" I asked.

"Once. In India. A guru with whom I was studying introduced me to an Indian-born immortal. He was many, many years past normal life expectancy and extremely spiritually aware. He could project his body anywhere and literally travel with his mind. I was in awe of his abilities. The only special ability I have is traveling out-of-body. I do this mostly to access the Akashic records. I can go into a trance and leave my body. Then, I will travel to the Akashic records and find out about my soul or another soul, such as yourself. By the way, do you want to know more about yourself?"

"Sure," I said, with excitement and anticipation. He had my attention. I couldn't help but stare intently into Peter's blue eyes.

"You have spent many lifetimes on this planet and have a close link to Jesus' era. You have been a Gnostic several times. That's why you are here now. You came back to help with the transition, and to see this era come to a successful conclusion. In some respects, you do not belong here because you are too advanced spiritually. In other words, you do not fit in, and you do not feel comfortable. However, you came to be a pillar, to show others the way to the truth. You are a lightworker."

I smiled. "That all makes sense."

"I understand why you are excited about the transition. Your life has not been easy, and you look forward to a time of more ease and tranquility. And once the transition begins, you look forward to sharing your awareness with others more openly. People like you and me will be helpful during the transition, helping others to understand what is happening.

"Your karmic role during your present reincarnation cycle has been that of a priest-scholar. You have only two more lifetimes to complete this cycle. Both of these lives will be on another planet in another galaxy. They will be pleasant lives, and you will feel an incredible amount of love and serenity.

"Your next reincarnation cycle will be that of an artisan. In all of the roles you have lived, you have never been an artisan or even had a sub-role as an artisan. Although you are using your creative abilities to write during this lifetime,

Chapter Two – Hopi Reservation Part 2

you now want to learn to make art and play music. There is a possibility of coming back to Earth during your next reincarnation cycle.

"About your past, John.... You have been a warrior, king, server, scholar, and, of course, a priest. You have been everything and experienced nearly everything, and lived over 1,000 lives on dozens of planets in several galaxies. You have completed four reincarnation cycles and are nearly finished with your fifth.

"Your spiritual awareness has made this current life difficult. Once you began to remember the truth in your late twenties, it was a painful jolt. All of a sudden, you understood things that few people could comprehend. This knowledge did not make your life easier. In fact, the new knowledge made your life more difficult, as you began to realize your predicament.

"You found yourself trapped on a planet where nearly everyone is hypnotized. What could you do? At first, you tried to tell people the good news, and you tried to explain the truth. You did not realize that your ability to remember the truth was inherent and that other people's ability to remember also was inherent. You learned that it all comes down to the level of spiritual awareness we have at birth. At this time, only certain people have the ability to remember the truth. Fortunately for us, that is now changing as the vibration of consciousness increases.

"Subsequently, you learned to keep your mouth shut. Once in a while, you have given someone a few bits of truth. But, over time, you have learned that few people can grasp even the basic concepts. It has been frustrating to keep your mouth shut, but you have learned to accept the situation. You have learned to relax and wait patiently for the transition.

"I could tell you about your future in this life, John, but I will not. It will be better for your life to be a mystery. You should figure it out on your own. Not even I know my own future. I have access only to my past. The guardians of the Akashic records will not let me see my future.

"I will tell you this, John. There is nothing for you to be afraid of in this lifetime. Keep your spirits up and walk with courage. Know that you are not alone and that you will be guided through any situation. Your life is protected."

Peter smiled and looked at me as if I were part of his family. I could tell he was finished.

I smiled. "Thank you for the reading. I know I have guides with me at all times. I never feel alone, and I constantly receive guidance. However, sometimes I can tell when they want me to figure it out and make my own decisions, or if it is too early to know something."

"Exactly," Peter said. "You create your life. Your guides can only help with certain events, and their help depends on how closely you pay attention to their guidance. They cannot create your life for you. That is for you to do. For instance, if you decide you want to be a hermit, they cannot change you into a gregarious socialite. If you decide you want to be single, they cannot find you a mate."

* * * * *

After Peter and I had talked for more than an hour, a Hopi man came into the room and asked if we were hungry. Peter looked at me, and I nodded. We rose and followed the Native Americans into another pueblo, where food was being cooked. There were two Hopi men seated and eating at a simple dining table. We joined them. They were in their twenties and dressed like typical Americans, with Levi's and

Chapter Two - Hopi Reservation Part 2

button-down shirts. Peter introduced them. "This is Paul and Steve."

I put out my hand. "Hello, I'm John Randall. Nice to meet you."

"Sorry you had to wait so long to see Peter," Paul said, as we shook hands. "We keep him protected. You're actually the first person from the outside who's been allowed to see him this month. We usually turn everyone away unless they have a good reason. By the way, I hear you're an author of spiritual books?"

"Yes," I said. "Are you interested in metaphysical spirituality?"

Peter interjected. "These two young men are old souls, John. Do not let their ages deceive you. They are very aware. I was surprised by their spiritual knowledge when I arrived here. It seems that the Hopi know a lot more than they announce. They are very secretive with their spiritual knowledge." Peter smiled.

"Was the comet in March 1997 the blue star?" I asked Paul.

"Hale-Bopp?" Steve asked.

"Yeah, do you think the Hale-Bopp comet was the blue star prophesied by your ancestors?"

"We're not supposed to talk about it with outsiders," Paul said, glancing sternly at Steve.

I looked at Steve. "What about The Book of Hopi? Wasn't it written by a Hopi elder? Also, there have been many lectures at the Whole Life Expo by Thomas Barranca and other prominent Hopis. This rule is not exactly unbroken."

"I'll talk," Steve said, glancing at Paul. "Peter seems to trust you. After all, we have talked with Peter at length about the prophecy. And you are correct, many Hopi have been releasing knowledge as we approach the end of the fourth world. Yes, we think Hale-Bopp was the blue star. The timing could not be a coincidence. It was expected less than a lifetime after the great explosions, which were the bombings of Hiroshima and Nagasaki. And it was fifty years later, so we were expecting the blue star to appear. The elders said Hale-Bopp was the blue star."

"What happens next?" I asked.

"After the blue star, a period of purification begins. Major earth changes, as well as economic and social problems will come. Then another major comet will appear in the sky. The second comet will actually be the sign of the impending demise of the fourth world. The blue star signified the beginning of the end.

"Since the blue star appeared," Steve continued, "people of the fourth world have been going through a period of initiation. Those who understand that a new era is upon us and choose to prepare will survive. Those who try to hang onto the customs and beliefs of the fourth world will not. The changes will be so significant that people will die if they do not change…"

"Can I interrupt?" I asked.

Steve nodded.

"Edna Frankel channeled the Circle of Grace meditation from the Brotherhood of Light and shared it with humanity on her web page. If this meditation is done on a daily basis, it keeps our aura clear and keeps us healthy. The Brotherhood said it is crucial for the coming changes. Is this something that will keep people from dying?"

Steve nodded. "Yes, any form of conscious energy work on the body will have a healing effect. This type of energy healing will be very important to protect the body. The energy vibration on the planet is going to change, which will affect our soul vibration and our energetic auras.

Chapter Two - Hopi Reservation Part 2

Many people will die from disease if they don't raise their vibration. Meditation and energy work will raise your vibration and keep people from getting sick."

Peter interjected. "Keeping our auras clear and unblocked will be very important. People don't realize how complex the aura is. There are four parts: physical, emotional, mental, and spiritual. Any one of these parts can be blocked and cause illness. This is why keeping the aura balanced is the key to good health. This is done through nutrition, meditation, exercise, and energy work, and will become common in metaphysical communities.

"While these daily practices are important, our thoughts are perhaps even more important. Our thoughts can easily put our aura out of balance. For instance, negative thoughts of revenge, anger, or hatred, will spill over into your aura. Conversely, thoughts of love and compassion will make your aura shine brightly. So, it is the combination of good practices and good thoughts that brings your soul into balance and gives you both good mental and physical health.

"What's important to understand is that we are energetic beings, and our energy field impacts our health. It is our personal responsibility to keep our energy in harmony and balance. This is becoming more important as the vibration of the planet increases."

Peter stopped and allowed Steve to continue. "The world is about to become a new place, with new ideas, new beliefs, and new healing modalities. The energy on the planet will be different. People with negative thoughts literally will die of their thoughts. I know that sounds strange, even bizarre. But the planet will no longer allow people to live on it who are not compatible with the new energy. Only people with spiritual awareness will be allowed to stay. Millions of people will die from illness. It will be easy to get sick during the great purification. However, if we have a pure heart and keep our aura clear, sickness will not harm us."

"This new world that you speak of ... will all the races live in harmony together?" I asked.

Steve nodded. "Yes. No longer will people live along racial lines. No longer will competition and power be the deciding factors in social structures. The new factors will be love, compassion, and an awareness that we are all equal. The present-day segregation of races will not be the norm in the future."

"I hold the same beliefs," I said. "It's refreshing to know that there are others who hold these beliefs. Your analysis of the current state of affairs must lead you to the conclusion that this planet will evolve soon. I agree. But how chaotic will this transition be?"

"Very!" Steve said passionately. "There are too many young souls in power and too many young souls in general. Young souls will have a difficult time adjusting to the new paradigm. They are here to learn about ego, which isn't conducive to the new paradigm. They won't be comfortable giving up their nice things, especially when we, the old souls, tell them that the world must change and become simpler. When we tell them that they must share, they will rebel. When we tell them the rules need to change, they will rebel.

"I don't see any possibility for an easy transition." Steve continued. "Although I do see a quick transition. It's going to be a strange period in history. Events will happen so rapidly that we won't get a chance to analyze what's happening. We'll just move on and forget about the events of last week or last month. When a college closes its doors, or a corporation goes out of business, we won't analyze or ponder the consequences anymore. We'll simply move on.

Chapter Two - Hopi Reservation Part 2

"The young souls will try to control the events, but the rapidity of change will outpace their efforts. 'Change' will be the watchword. Eventually, economic and social trauma will spur spiritual change. For instance, new social structures and new ways of living will appear. Before anyone realizes the impact of the changes, it will be too late to do anything to stop them. Those who wish to hold onto old beliefs will be outnumbered. New beliefs and new ideas will be in the forefront. A New Age will be dawning."

"The Age of Aquarius?" I asked.

Steve nodded. "Yeah. Astrologers know that the Age of Aquarius begins sometime soon. They can't give an exact date, but they know the Age of Pisces is in its last years. I think we have entered the cusp period, where both energies are impacting humanity. We're going to experience an incredible transition over the next few decades. Hold on to your bootstraps."

I laughed. "I have them tied tight, trust me."

We all laughed.

After we finished eating, I said goodbye to Peter and his friends. Peter said he would be ready for the trip when I returned in two weeks. I gave him the tour itinerary as well as the date and time when I would be back to get him. It had been an incredible day, and I was really looking forward to our trip.

CHAPTER THREE

Los Angeles Lecture

Two weeks later, I picked Peter up from the Hopi Reservation in my Honda Civic. We had a long, nine-hour drive to the Hilton Hotel near the Los Angeles International Airport. He strode to the car wearing cargo shorts, sandals, and an un-tucked casual t-shirt. I carried his suitcase and placed it in the back of the hatchback.

"Is this how all immortals dress?" I asked.

Peter smiled. "No one cares how you dress in this country. I paid ten dollars for these rubber sandals, and just like me, they never wear out."

I laughed at his joke.

I was also wearing shorts, but mine were new. My shirt was button-down and tucked in. Neither my shorts nor my shirt were wrinkled. I couldn't say the same for Peter's. We got into the car and headed down the road.

"Good thing you have a small car," Peter said. "Peak oil has made gasoline expensive."

"I've heard of peak oil, but how would you define it?" I asked, as we started off.

"Peak oil is when global oil production begins to decline. At that point, oil supply will no longer meet demand at an affordable price. Basically, it is the end of cheap energy, and the end of this era's growth economy. We are getting close. It should be somewhere around one hundred million barrels per day. Once we reach the peak, production will begin to decline.

"Graphically, it looks like a bell curve. As production increases, the bell curve increases upwards. Eventually, the apex of the curve is reached. This apex is peak oil. Once we reach the apex, it is downhill from there. Never again will we produce as much oil."

"You are full of information," I said. "I guess we will have plenty to talk about on this trip."

Peter smiled. "Indeed. Do you want to hear more about peak oil?"

I nodded. "Sure.

"Cheap energy is about to go bye-bye. That will obliterate the economy. Without affordable energy, the economy cannot grow. We are literally in the last days of the American empire. Your standard of living is about to collapse."

I glanced at Peter. "That's not exactly a surprise to me. It's what I expect. I've always known a collapse is where we are headed, and that life is going to become hyper-localized. We will eat local food, get our energy locally, work for local companies, and even govern ourselves locally."

"You are right about that, John. Once the energy crisis destroys the corporations, people will have no choice but to develop a localized economy. Actually, it might not be oil that brings us down first. It might be the death of the dollar, and then peak oil will finish us off economically.

I smiled, realizing that we were in agreement. "I agree. I've always thought it would be the collapse of the financial system that destroyed the economy, and not high energy prices. I've followed the dollar and unemployment rates more closely than the price of oil."

Chapter Three - Los Angeles Lecture

"John, don't underestimate the impact of oil. Before we began pumping oil out of the ground in the nineteenth century, there were one billion people on the planet. Once we harnessed cheap energy, the industrial revolution occurred, and the global population exploded. Do you realize that 20 percent of all fossil fuel is used by the food industry? That estimate is probably high, but less oil means less food."

"Oh, I understand the magnitude of peak oil," I said. "It is the lifeblood of the economy. Without affordable energy, and everything grinds to a halt. However, the crisis of the dollar seems more dire to me in the short term. It has gotten so bad that I wish I had all of my investments in gold."

Peter laughed. "You got that right! Most people agree that gold is the best asset to own in a crisis. They just never thought we would have a crisis like this! However, this is not a dollar crisis but a debt crisis. The financial system in America is insolvent, and the U.S. Government is trying to borrow its way out, which everyone knows is impossible. All they are doing is adding more debt to a debt problem. The end result is the death of the dollar and a run to gold."

I nodded and fell silent, mulling over his words as I drove.

* * * * *

The next day, we were scheduled to give our L.A. lecture at 2 p.m. We arrived on time to a sold-out room of approximately two hundred and fifty people. Many had read one of my books or had been referred by someone who had. They came to hear me speak, but I was perfectly comfortable sharing the podium with Peter. Music from Van Morrison played on a Sony portable stereo, at the front of the room. I always arranged to have music playing for the people who arrived early to set the tone.

Peter and I walked to the front of the room. I turned off the stereo and approached the lectern. "Hello, I'm John Randall," I announced to the large audience. "Thanks for coming. Today, I will be sharing the podium with Peter Vaughn, an enlightened teacher. I think you will enjoy listening to him. Without wasting time with introductions, we will begin. Peter will speak first and then I will follow. Afterward, we will both take questions. Here is Peter."

I held out my arm in a welcoming gesture as Peter strode to the lectern.

"Hello, thank you all for coming. As John told you, my name is Peter Vaughn. I hope my speech is informative. Today, I want to talk about the current state of spiritual awareness. This is an important subject because it is the very foundation of our culture and society. It is also important because it will determine our future. Our fate is literally tied to our spiritual awareness. Why? Because what we believe defines who we are."

Peter paused and scanned the audience.

"As a caveat, John and I may sound dogmatic with some of our ideas and beliefs. So, please do not accept everything we say as the only possible version of the truth. Who is to say if John or I are correct? Certainly not us. We do not propose to know the definitive truth. We suggest that you consider all diverse ideas and beliefs, and come to your own version of the truth. Our goal here is nothing more than to inspire you to search out additional ideas and come to your own conclusions."

Peter paused for a moment to contemplate. "Accepting what we have to say as dogma would be counter to our goal of public speaking. We do not feel that the future will be

Chapter Three - Los Angeles Lecture

based on dogma. We envision a civilization where spiritually aware people will hold their own personal beliefs. When dogma is held by groups of people, it creates division. So, the last thing we want is to form a group that agrees with all of our beliefs.

"For those of you experienced in metaphysics, many of our comments you will have heard before, although we might define a concept differently than your understanding. However, do not think that we are here to tell you that our version is the correct version of the truth. We will share our ideas and beliefs, and you can take what you want. Compare, synthesize, and collect beliefs. Never accept one version as the definitive truth. Find your own."

Peter paused and grinned, and many in the audience smiled back. "Okay, let's start. For the vast majority in this country, the current state of spiritual awareness is that of ignorance and naïveté. This vast majority lacks understanding. This lack of understanding was so pervasive that the humanity's survival was threatened. Thankfully, the mass consciousness has now evolved to a point where that won't happen. In fact, it is time to celebrate because we have reached a threshold were spiritual change is now our destiny. A change of epic proportions is about to occur. I call this period of change 'the transition,' others call it 'the great shift.' This transition will lead to a new civilization, one that is not based on power and conflict. Instead, this new civilization will be based on love and harmony.

"Many of you are wondering, what is this naïveté of the vast majority? What is this ignorance that threatened humanity's survival? The answer is obvious for most in this room: separation is a lie, and duality is a lie. There is no good and evil, there is no right or wrong, there is no you and me."

Someone in the room gasped.

Peter smiled. "Sorry for the red pill. Sometimes the truth can be jarring. The truth is simple. There is only one consciousness, which is the Creator. We all share that consciousness, and we are all aspects of the Creator. There is no separation between us the the Creator, nor between each other."

Peter paused and scanned the audience. "That's the truth that will be the foundation of the next civilization, as incredible as that sounds. So, now for the bad news. People are unaware of their inherent divinity. People are pretending that they are *not* God. They are pretending to be separate from God. This pretense will not last much longer, but it won't come without growing pains, as people hold onto their old false beliefs. It will split apart families. It will split apart friendships."

Peter paused again and stared at the audience. "God is our soul. It is who we are. We think we are separate from God. We are not. And when we deny our divinity, we act from fear and ignorance. In fact, the only blasphemy is the denial of the divine. Moreover, life becomes a complete mess once we deny our divinity. Why? Because at that point, we are living a lie. Our denial becomes the basis of everything we do. Life becomes a charade, with no meaning other than trying to find the truth."

Peter paused. "We are not from here. This is not our home. We incarnated on this planet to experience life from a different perspective, a perspective of separation and duality. But believe me, it is an illusionary perspective. We are all God playing this charade together. The good news is that the time has come to wake up to this illusion and grasp the truth.

"Separation and duality are nothing more than an illusion, and these strongly held beliefs are starting to change.

Chapter Three - Los Angeles Lecture

Everywhere around the world spiritual awareness is rapidly evolving. We are seeing an increase in compassion around the world. After the 9/11 attack, even the people in Iran held a public demonstration of sympathy for the victims. Instead of burning our flag, they waved it. Humanity is starting to come together.

"The most powerful thought that we can now have is that of compassion. Once we become enlightened, we have complete compassion for both ourselves and everyone with whom we interact. Compassion is what keeps us connected to our higher self, and to everyone else. As compassion grows on this planet, spiritual awareness will also grow. Steadily, the illusion of separation will fade. Soon we will stop pretending to be separate from one another and will begin to love each other. This will represent a revolutionary change in our belief systems.

"Currently, only a small minority of people are aware of their inherent divinity and the illusion of separateness. The people in this room, the New Agers or lightworkers, however you want to call yourselves, are aware of this fact and are leading the way for others to follow. Even though we know this to be true - that we are one - we do not force our beliefs upon others. Instead, we allow others to hold their own beliefs and to make their own choices. We know that they have their reasons for their beliefs and choices, and we honor those choices. We have a saying in the New Age movement that 'Everyone has their own path.' How someone chooses to live their life is their free choice. As I like to say, all experiences are valid."

Peter took a drink of water and then continued. "Those who are spiritually aware define love in compassionate terms. Some lightworkers define love as the lack of fear. I prefer the definition of love as the recognition of our inherent divinity, which leads to a profound respect for others, and a corresponding compassion for ourselves and others.

"The vast majority currently defines love differently. Today, love is generally equated with an emotional feeling towards another. However, without that emotion, compassion fades away. Most people today choose whom they love based on how they feel towards another. Unfortunately, most of those feelings are created by cultural conditioning. We are literally taught whom to love. Thus, our compassion is quite limited.

"I'll give an example, although I think all of you know what I am talking about. Recently, a conservative affluent family held a dinner party for a variety of friends. One of the guests made a comment about how the rich seem to have a better deal in America, and that they get all the breaks, whereas the middle class gets squeezed, and the lower class gets the bread crumbs. The host of the party became upset and said, 'You probably believe in socialism and in the redistribution of wealth.' The friend nodded and replied, 'Yes I do.' The host got angry and told his guest to please leave, and that they were not welcome here.

"I would use his colorful language, but this is a G-rated event today."

The audience laughed.

"That is the epitome of conditional love, and love based on emotion. Thus, with this belief, if you don't like someone, it is impossible to love them. This friend was literally ostracized in public by another friend, and was basically told that he was no longer loved. In fact, he was hated, simply for holding an opinion on our economic and political system. Amazingly, but that actually happened recently. And it happens every day. People go around loving and hating on little whims of emotion and false beliefs.

Chapter Three – Los Angeles Lecture

"Love, however, is not a feeling or an emotion, although love can be emotional. Love is who we are. It is the core of our being. It is the core of the Creator. Feelings that we have for others are the result of love. Love can cause emotion, but it is not the emotion itself. Emotions are the result of love, not vice versa.

"We do not get to choose whom we love. What we do get to choose is who brings out our emotions and which emotions we want to experience. The fact is, we love everyone, because everyone is us. To say that you do not love another is to deny divinity. And that is what this current civilization is about – denial, which is a lie. We are pretending to be something we are not – separate from one another."

Peter gestured with his hands. "How much longer will this pretense last? I do not know that answer, but I do know that it will not be very long. This is evidenced by the current state of affairs. As a nation, America has become affluent while disregarding equity. The rich get richer, and the lower class has been left behind. This has created an inequitable situation in society. And those who have been left behind are quite aware of the situation. There are millions of people who perceive that they are not being treated fairly. This resentment is going to show itself soon. This will lead to riots and looting in the major cities.

"Yes, many people are becoming more spiritually aware, and this is leading to an outbreak of love and compassion. However, this is a double-edged sword. As more people sense their inherent divinity, they cannot accept subjugation and inequality. Spiritual awareness gives people courage. This will lead to riots and crime. I just hope that these incidents are controlled and isolated.

"Once the economy fails and there are fewer jobs, things could very well turn violent in this country for a short period. With the increasing spiritual awareness on the planet, the 'have nots' are going to demand that they be treated as equals. Not with the quasi-equality that exists today, where the affluent have all the advantages and a life of luxury because of their access to money.

"We could prevent this situation from arising. All we would have to do, as a nation, is recognize our oneness. We could recognize the inequity that exists between the upper and lower classes. We could attempt to make the inner-city schools as good as suburban schools. We could show the less fortunate that we care about equity and fairness. We could look at the number of Black males in custody and realize that something is wrong. We could look at dropout rates and illiteracy rates. I do not think we will, however. I think the opportunity to save this country has already passed. I no longer think there are any political solutions. When we killed JFK, that marked the end. That was a sad day. That was the end of innocence for America.

"The 1960s were are our hope, and it died. America has been steadily dying every since, and now we approach it's demise and breakup.

"It is ironic that, as a nation, we cannot see that it is in our own self-interest to be equitable. We will look back in hindsight and see how spiritually ignorant we were. Yes, I am implying that it is a foregone conclusion. We could prevent all of this from happening by being more spiritually aware. However, we would have to recognize our inherent connection with one another, and that is not likely without a period of chaotic change.

"Change is imminent, and to a large extent, it is our own fault. However, please know that we are going to create

Chapter Three - Los Angeles Lecture

something better, and it is going to begin during *our* lifetime. The individual choices that we make in the near future will have an impact on the outcome of humanity's future. The current prevalent beliefs have created the disharmony that we face today, and those beliefs must change and *will* change. This change is what the transition is all about. And *we* are going to create this change.

"In the near future, when the transition begins in earnest, there will be a struggle between people who are aware that beliefs need to change, and those who attempt to hold onto the beliefs of the past to maintain the status quo. During this struggle, the prevalent belief systems will begin to shift and transform. As spiritual awareness increases, the general population will inevitably reflect this change. People will become more compassionate and more aware of their divinity, and old belief systems will begin to fade."

Peter paused and scanned the audience. "I know that it sounds utopian, but it is going to happen, and soon. The coming transition will reveal the fallacy and falsity of this nation's current beliefs. For instance, how will we treat the unemployed when the economic crisis begins? What human rights will we display? If the current beliefs remain, which is a likely scenario in the near term, people will be forced out of their homes and left homeless. Conversely, we could use new beliefs and begin to treat everyone humanely. The decisions we will be required to make are not that far away.

"I submit to you that the old belief systems are not going to work to help humanity move forward and we will begin to accept new beliefs. These new beliefs will actually be based on truth, whereas the old beliefs were based on fallacy, that we are separate from each other.

"That man who told his friend to leave his house and never come back is a good example of the decisions that are being made today. His cold, heartless decision came from fear. He is afraid that the status quo is breaking down and that he is losing his way of life. It's extraordinary how a country of America's affluence is on the precipice of losing its wealth, while at the same time facing a spiritual test on how it does it humanely."

Peter smiled. "God has quite the sense of humor. We have created this incredible society of affluence, and now it is going to be stripped away. During this transition, we will move toward a simpler, less affluent society. The challenges, as you can imagine, are going to be profound and difficult. However, they all have the same theme: How do you become more compassionate and loving towards your fellow human beings? Although that is the theme, there is actually a goal. The goal is finding an affinity with other human beings. Not just some humans, but all of them."

Peter paused. "You can imagine the problem we face. Humans don't like change, and this is a change of enormous magnitude. Although this room is full of lightworkers, we are the minority. The vast majority of people in this country believe they are separate from God and, therefore, separate from each other. This is why we have neglected the homeless and the impoverished. We have no affinity with these groups. No one believes that we have a commonality with each other, which is the opposite of the truth. Just because such ideas as the belief in separation are widely held does not mean they represent the truth. Instead, it is just a reality that we have all collectively invented. This is how current beliefs have created the ignorance that exists today.

"When the economic crisis begins, and America begins to flounder, many people will begin to understand that beliefs are the crux of the problem and that new ideas and new beliefs are needed. A struggle will ensue between

Chapter Three - Los Angeles Lecture

the people with new ideas and beliefs and those who still believe in separation and the status quo. This struggle will be spiritual in nature. It will be a struggle for power and for the right to determine the foundation for future of humanity.

"Everything chaotic that is going to happen in the near future can be attributed to spiritual ignorance. That is why I talk about spirituality. It is our level of spirituality that has created the disharmony that exists today. In other words, it is not the devil, but simply our current collective beliefs that have created the negative aspects of society."

Peter took a drink from his bottle of water. "We are about to go through a transition period. This chaotic period of the transition will last about one generation, although it will take four generations to expunge all of our false beliefs. The currently accepted belief that we are separate will be supplanted by the belief that we are all *one*. This is such a huge change from the current belief in separation that it can be considered a spiritual transformation. Indeed, in twenty years, civilization will barely resemble how we live today. And, in fifty years, it will not resemble today in the slightest degree. People will look back on our current civilization with disdain and pity, or possibly just indifference. Our current culture will be remembered as a period of spiritual ignorance, a period to be forgotten."

Peter paused. "God is *all*. God is *everyone* and *everything*. Everything is alive and everything is conscious. Everything is connected. Everything is God. When we ignore these truths and treat people with disdain and indifference, we create disharmony. We have created a myriad of disharmony. This is obvious. All you have to do is spend one night in an emergency room in a large U.S. city to see the evidence: drug and alcohol abuse, spousal abuse, child abuse, gang warfare, and other forms of violence. It is easy to see that a new form of society would be a welcome change. When enough people come to this conclusion, the world will change. Thank you."

Peter turned and walked toward me. The crowd politely applauded. I applauded also and grinned as he sat next to me.

I looked at Peter. "Well done."

Peter grinned. "Thanks."

I rose and approached the lectern and faced the audience.

"Hello, everyone. As you may know, my name is John Randall. Thank you for coming. Today, I will talk about soul growth and reincarnation. Because I have only thirty minutes, I can only give an overview. Hopefully, however, it will be interesting. Once I am finished, Peter and I will answer your questions.

"Let's start with a question. How many of you think you are a distinct entity, separate from the rest of the people in this room?" I waited for the show of hands, but no one raised theirs. "Surprisingly, the majority of Americans believe that we are separate from each other. In fact, as Peter just announced, we are all *one*. There is no distinct separation between anything. The truth is that any separation we perceive is an illusion. When we look at someone else, we are seeing another aspect of ourselves. For, our soul and our consciousness, which is the same thing, originate at the same source, which is God's consciousness."

I paused and scanned the room. "God didn't create us as distinct separate entities apart from Itself. Why? Because God can't create something from nothing. If God wants to create something, God must create from Itself. Whatever God decides to create becomes an extension of Itself.

"The question arises, are God's creations *God*? If so, how many of God's attributes can God give to Its creations?

Chapter Three - Los Angeles Lecture

Can God create other gods? For those of you who think this can't be done, consider your beliefs. You're saying that you know what God can and cannot create. If God can create the universe, don't you think that God can create other gods as well? In fact, God has. Look at someone in this room, and you're observing a god-in-training, a god created by God. Yes, we are each an imitation of God, with many of the same attributes.

"Each of us is in training. We're learning to use the attributes inherent in our being. When we die, and our soul leaves our body, we get a glimpse of these inherent attributes as our soul acclimates to the etheric world of spirit. We have a sense of wonder that is incredible. The etheric world is quite the opposite of this physical planet, which is very dense. A veil separates the world of the physical from the world of the etheric. While incarnate on this planet, most of us cannot see through this veil.

"Why does this veil exist? The only way our soul can evolve and become like God is to experience from a context of amnesia. God created the physical plane specifically for our evolution. This is why we have forgotten who we really are. Once we remember, the illusion of the veil becomes apparent, and we can travel and communicate through it. This is why soul travel and channeling are so common today.

"Why did God create the physical world? Think for a moment from a logical point of view. God is a creator. God created the universe and everything in the universe. Yet, why create things? Just to see what God could create? Just to watch Its creations? No. Life is much more complex than that. God wanted to see Its creations come to life and evolve through experience. Experience and evolvement give meaning to creations.

"God wants to see what can *emerge* from Its creations. We're special creations because we've been blessed with God's abilities. As we evolve, we're actually becoming gods. We actually will evolve to a point where we can create just like God created. Interesting thought, isn't it? And it's *true*.

"This brings us to the topic of reincarnation. If our soul is going to use the physical plane to learn to become like God, then reincarnation is required. One lifetime surely would not be sufficient. Currently, only a minority of Americans believe in reincarnation. It's amazing how ignorant we are about reality. Each of us has reincarnated into a physical body hundreds or thousands of times. Yet many people think this is their first and last life in a physical form. As the old saying goes, 'I would believe in reincarnation, if I could remember my last life.'" A few people in the audience laughed.

"When we are in Heaven, and we decide to incarnate and experience the physical plane, we know that it is for *our* benefit and that the experiences will be beneficial. We know in advance what can happen and what potential learning experiences can occur. For instance, when someone is born with a disability, it isn't a tragedy. It was created as a learning experience. My point is all experiences are valid and beneficial. Not just experiences that we deem acceptable, but *all* experiences.

"From our limited awareness, we are in no position to judge right or wrong, good or bad, perfect or imperfect. Our true identity is so much vaster than we realize. We are here to evolve, and how that is attained is inconsequential. If you cringe and rebel against this idea, then you are stuck in the paradigm of separation. In a future lifetime, you will recognize your divinity and see the naiveté in judging another, judging yourself, or judging God."

Chapter Three - Los Angeles Lecture

I stopped for a moment to take a drink from my water bottle. "Peter mentioned the current pervasive belief in separation. I call this the paradigm of separation, which is how we live today. This paradigm causes society to constantly judge behavior. Judgment usually begins with morality, but then expands to include nearly every aspect of life. Instead of allowing us to live as we want, society constantly judges our behavior.

"How we treat each other, how we live our lives, even how we decorate our homes, all become fodder for societal judgment. Turn on the television and you will constantly see people nitpicking over what is acceptable and what isn't. The degree of judgment has gotten so out of hand that it is almost impossible not to be criticized by half the people you know." The audience laughed at my slight exaggeration.

"Life is complicated in a paradigm of separation. No one knows who to trust or what to believe. We end up playing follow the leader and affiliating with groups who we identify with. And without knowledge of our higher self, fear becomes pervasive. Our base instincts of power, security, and hedonism become dominant. Society inevitably degenerates into a chaotic mess, which is what we have created.

"If it wasn't for reincarnation, I would be concerned about the future. However, reincarnation allows God to put plans in motion. For instance, each of us has our own agenda. This is called our reincarnation blueprint. Reincarnation allows us to determine in advance which experiences we want to have. We literally can decide what we want to learn. We can choose from a myriad of variables that will be at play during our lives. For instance, we can choose hundreds of variables that make up our emotional, mental, and psychological attributes. We can choose what we will look like, whom we will be attracted to, whom we will be compatible with, and so on.

"The intricacies of our lives would astound us if we could perceive them, with much of them predetermined before we were born. Astrology is perhaps the best example that reveals the array of attributes from which we can choose. A good astrologer has an idea of the complexity of choices available to us before we incarnate.

"Besides our emotional, mental, and psychological attributes, there are other factors as well. For instance, we choose what lessons we want to learn and with whom we wish to learn them. These lessons can have an array of characteristics. We can learn major lessons, minor lessons, or combinations. We can learn how to care for a disabled person or how to live with a disability ourselves. We can learn to lead people or to take orders. We can learn to make things. We can learn how to have relationships. As you can imagine, there are many choices. Everyone comes here with a life lesson that was determined before they take their first breath."

I took another drink of water. "Reincarnation is actually a well-defined system of rules and procedures. As complex as our lives are, everything occurs within a controlled system. For instance, each of us is currently completing a reincarnation cycle. Within this cycle, we must complete a series of stages and lessons. In fact, the only way we can incarnate on the physical plane is to agree to complete a reincarnation cycle. We can't just decide that we want to live one life on a planet. Using incarnations to evolve our soul is a serious decision. It's a commitment that we have to honor.

"The reincarnation cycle is as follows.[1] First, we select a role. This role will be the basis of our personality, and we will live one entire reincarnation cycle in the same role. This

Chapter Three - Los Angeles Lecture

cycle can last anywhere from thirty-five to five hundred lives, with an average of approximately one hundred and twenty-five lives.

"The following are the seven roles from which we can choose. I will name them first and then describe each one." I recited the list slowly. "There's King, Priest, Warrior, Artisan, Scholar, Sage, and Server.

"A *king* is a leader and generally has a throne of some kind (in other words, a family, business, organization, and so on).

"A *priest* learns and teaches about spirituality.

"A *warrior* is action-oriented; most good workers and athletes are warriors.

"An *artisan* creates – anything from art, music, or writing to surgery.

"*Scholars* teach, learn, and distribute knowledge.

"A *sage* is someone who is expressive and communicative. Sages are actors, entertainers, and comedians.

"*Servers* help others and society in some sort of service or support role.

"In addition, each role is also broken into stages and levels. At each level, we learn lessons that apply to that level. Currently, I am a fifth-level, old soul priest. That is why I can stand here and talk about spirituality without notes. I have lived so many lives learning about spirituality that it comes easily to me.

"Now, what do I mean by fifth level, old soul priest? My role is a priest, and I am in the old soul stage, and at the fifth level of that stage.

"There are five stages that we must pass through. These stages are on a continuum, with the first stage having very little spiritual awareness, to the last stage, which ends with enlightenment.

"At the *infant* stage, which is the first stage, we learn survival lessons.

"At the *baby* stage, we learn how to follow directions and how to assimilate into a group.

"At the *young* stage, we learn lessons of the ego, where we become preoccupied with our own identity.

"At the *mature* stage, we learn lessons about our emotions. Here, relationships are paramount, and traumas and dramas are common.

"At the *old* stage, which is the last stage, we learn lessons about spirituality and unconditional love. This results in spiritual enlightenment.

"When we begin a cycle, we start at the first level of the infant stage, where we live a series of lives. Steadily, we advance up the seven levels of the infant stage until we progress to the baby stage. We continue with all the levels of each stage in the same manner. It normally requires more than one lifetime at each level.

"The average person on the planet has completed three cycles. That means the average person has incarnated more than three hundred times. Myself, I have incarnated over a thousand, and I have experienced nearly everything." I grinned. "I know now that there is no reason to judge behavior and that experiences are for learning, not condemnation. The reincarnation cycle was established specifically to experience *everything*. This is God's way of experiencing the infinite."

I stopped briefly and took another drink of water. "Old souls tend to understand that the only thing that matters is love. For them, life is about love. They learn how to love themselves and how to love others as they love themselves.

Chapter Three - Los Angeles Lecture

This is the last lesson. It is the last one before we remember our divinity and become enlightened. The saying that 'God is love' is true. That's why this lesson is last. That's also why compassion is the most powerful thought you can have. Compassion is the direct result of unconditional love.

"Unconditional love is the last lesson, but not all souls are ready for the God lesson. Young souls are fixated on their own identities; they are unable to love others as they love themselves. Instead, they view others as competitors. Most self-made millionaires, CEOs, and politicians are young souls. They are ambitious and ego-driven, and often have no conscience.

"I mention them because young souls are currently the elite in our society. They have become the elite because we live in a power-based culture under our paradigm of separation. Power accrues from money, which young souls are adept at obtaining. When society begins to transform into a humane, love-based culture, old souls will begin to have influence, especially old soul women."

I noticed the women in the audience quietly smiling and nodding.

"Do you see how reincarnation creates the complexity of life? We have all these roles and levels, and lessons, and horoscopes and cycles, and the list goes on and on. How could all of this complexity possibly be organized? The answer, of course, is God. God intermeshes and intertwines everything together because God is consciously connected to everything. God can know what everyone is thinking and doing. God literally can control everything by being everything. God's omnipresence is a reality. God can hear your thoughts, and God can influence your decisions. Thus, you are not self-contained, and you are not alone. In fact, you are never alone.

"Think about it. I know it's a deep thought, but think about it. Can God really control everything by being everything? The answer is yes. God created us to experience life *interactively*. God provides us with enough ability to live on our own using free choice, while at the same time influencing us. For this reason, our choices are limited, and free will is actually constrained.

"Think of a robot as an analogy. We program a robot to vacuum the floor. At the same time, we can use a remote control to override its programming. In a way, that's how God influences us. We have free will to a certain extent, and then events happen that make us shudder with awe at the omniscient overtones."

I paused briefly to give the audience a moment to think.

"For instance, how often does a favorable event happen in your life that you can't explain? Or events that, in hindsight, ended up being providential?

"The following is a true event that happened in my life. If this wasn't the hand of God, then I don't know what is. On April 4, 2004, I stopped on my way to the mountains to get a fishing license. The license number was 44. I thought, cool, that is a good omen. On my last day in the mountains, I wanted to leave early, but I needed to help my Uncle Norman fix the well pump. I remember looking at my watch and wanting to leave, but the urge to stay and finish the job was even stronger. Finally, we finished at 5 p.m. By then, dinner was almost ready, so I stayed. It was tacos, which is my favorite. After dinner, my niece and nephew asked me to stay one more night and go home in the morning, but I had a strong urge to go home.

"When I got close enough to town, my cell phone beeped for incoming voicemail messages once I was within range of a cell tower. I listened to them and was offered a fantastic

Chapter Three - Los Angeles Lecture

job that I had interviewed for. I had been disappointed all weekend because I thought I didn't get it. That job lasted from 2004 to 2016 and was incredibly fulfilling and lucrative.

Another message was from Bernie, to call him back about a Rod Stewart concert. I figured I had missed that. It was already nearly 8 p.m. when I got home, and my mother said that Bernie had just called. I called him back, thinking that I was going to say no. He answered from the concert, and I was thinking of excuses, when he handed the phone to Jorge, one of my best friends. Just hearing Jorge's voice changed my entire demeanor. Now I *wanted* to go.

"I asked if there was room for me, and Jorge said, 'Yes, just get a ticket and come to the suite.' I drove to the concert, and when I arrived, there were very few people outside. I asked the first person I saw where I could get a ticket. He handed me one for free and said that he worked for the radio station. I walked into the building, and as I handed my ticket to the doorman, I saw a friend walking past. I called her name. Synchronistically, she was on her way to Bernie's suite and showed me the way. We arrived, and there were two of my best friends, Jorge and Bernie. Incredibly, I arrived at intermission, just prior to Rod Stewart taking the stage. The concert was fantastic, and we had a memorable time. Throughout the concert, I was smiling for two reasons. One, I was with the people I loved, and we were having a great time. And two, I felt that the hand of God had brought us together.

"I learned long ago that there are forces in my life that are stronger than I am. I don't know about you, but I listen to my heart and attempt to be as honest as I can, both with myself and others. I know, from experience, that forces out of my control will dictate my experiences, especially if I try to control my life. I gave up trying to do that long ago."

I paused to let this thought reach everyone. "The greatest gift that God gave us is the ability of our soul to evolve. That's why I said earlier that we're learning to become gods. This isn't exactly true, because we already *are* God, or at least in some way directly connected. Make no mistake: There is no separation between us and God. However, that doesn't mean that our souls can't evolve. We can evolve to an incredible degree, becoming as god-like as we can imagine."

I paused again. "You may be thinking, if we are one with God, do we truly exist as individuals? Is our soul, which is evolving through our diligence, truly our own? The answer is 'No.' We don't really exist as individuals. Individuality is an illusion. This is why advanced souls focus on selflessness, compassion, and sensitivity towards others. The more advanced you become, the less your individuality matters.

"Knowing that your soul is not really yours, is that going to make you mad at God and perhaps rebellious, and refuse to evolve? Surprisingly, many souls do rebel. Anyone heard of Satan?" The audience laughed lightheartedly.

"Rebellion is normal. Most of the people on this planet are rebelling against God. Instead of living the values of God, and everyone knows what those are, most people are selfish and rebellious. As the Cindy Lauper song says it so well, 'Girls just wanna have fun.' It could also have been written for men. Perpetually seeking fun is not devotion to God. That's hedonism, nihilism, and selfishness, and it occurs through free will. Look at the addictions in this country to alcohol and drugs. That's rebellion at its best."

I took another drink of water. "Devotion or fun? God definitely gives us a choice. The route to devotion is littered with deviations and misdirection. It is a path we are all on. You can see why God must have a sense of humor. He knows it is an arduous journey.

Chapter Three - Los Angeles Lecture

"Oh yes, rebellion is rampant. But is it futile? Yes, and that is the beauty of God. We can rebel all we want, but in the end, God leads us back home. Maybe not this lifetime, but we all eventually evolve. That is what reincarnation is all about. Each life is planned in advance, and the results do lead to the next life. Some of us are expert rebellers, taking several lifetimes just to learn one lesson. But eventually, we all become god-like and learn to love ourselves and our fellow humans. Everyone learns the last lesson, which is unconditional love.

"If everyone is going to learn the last lesson, then rebellion is not wrong. It is our choice. Whatever we choose to do can lead only to our benefit; nothing can detract from our evolvement. We can do whatever we want, and we will still evolve. Contrary to common wisdom, we can't make mistakes – no matter how severe – without benefiting from them.

"The question arises, why is evolution so difficult? Why do we have to struggle so much to get to the last lesson? The answer is, we make it difficult. We want to experience the good and the bad. Most of us *want* a challenge. And I'll tell you right now, as if you didn't know, life is quite a challenge." A ripple of laughter ensued.

I looked at my watch and noticed that nearly an hour had passed. "Okay, it's time for questions. There's a microphone in the front."

I pointed in the direction of the microphone, which was placed at the front of the aisle. Peter joined me at the lectern. Several people rose and made their way to the front.

First was a young woman holding an infant in her arms. "You make it sound as if everything is perfect," she said, "as if all our pain and trauma were little more than learning experiences, and as if the sin that occurs on a daily basis were perfectly all right, pun intended."

I looked at Peter and smiled. "You should answer. I already did, and she doesn't believe me." I stepped back from the lectern, and many in the audience laughed softly to relieve the tension.

"That is a beautiful baby you have," Peter said to the young mother. "You can go sit down, and I will answer your question."

"Thank you," she said, returning to her seat.

"What John was talking about is *truth*," Peter said. "This truth is new for most people and not yet widely known. In time, people will come to understand that we are all *one*. Until then, people will continue to believe in right and wrong, good and evil.

"Currently, conventional wisdom decrees what is good and what is bad. In effect, people are conditioned into accepting such ideas. Moreover, they end up hardened and judgmental, lacking the compassion that Jesus preached.

"I will give you an example. I was at a restaurant recently, and a homeless woman came in and sat down at my table. She told me not to pay any attention to her, that she would not be there long. She quickly examined the room with a sense of foreboding and remained seated for about ten seconds. Suddenly, she rose and left the room.

"A restaurant employee approached and asked if a homeless woman had come in from the outside. I answered yes. His facial expression changed to reveal his anxiety, and he hurried after her as if she were a criminal.

"The people at the next table started laughing. They asked me what happened to my date and made other jokes, such as, 'She was starting to like you.' The homeless lady was a pariah. She was being judged as lacking essential

Chapter Three - Los Angeles Lecture

human traits and was subsequently considered not their equal. The people at the next table were mostly middle-aged women. I do not think they all wanted to laugh. However, once the jokes started, each person at the table joined in. I remember how much joy they had in making fun of another human being.

"This is where our current beliefs have gotten us. We laugh at other human beings who are in intense emotional pain. We take away from them the very thing that they need most, which is dignity, love, and compassion. Why? Because they are deemed to be a bad influence on society. Under our current standards, anything that is perceived as bad is open to criticism."

Peter stepped back, and I approached the lectern. "Next question?"

The next person in line, a young man, said, "I was going to ask about young souls and old souls, but the last answer got my attention. Peter said something about a *new* truth. That's an interesting concept. Was he implying there is a specific truth, and that this generation is going to find it?"

I turned back to Peter. "This is for you, too."

Peter approached the lectern again, and I stepped aside. Peter said to the man, "Yes, there will be a new truth for *this* generation. However, there is nothing new under the sun. It is a matter of the majority becoming spiritually aware of remembering *old* truth. Yes, there is truth. Why wouldn't there be? As ordered as the universe is, there is also order in our lives. Think of the miracle of the human body. The mind that created our bodies can also create order in our lives and can help us discover the *truth* about our lives.

"Out of truth, comes order. Order comes from an understanding and an awareness of spiritual truth. This civilization has not been fully exposed to this truth because it has not been appropriate. In the near future, this knowledge will be released, and spiritual awareness will unfold. It is our destiny.

"Over the next generation, millions of people will learn and understand the truth. To answer your question, yes, this generation will find the truth. And with imagination, you can fathom the implications. Everything is going to change for the better. Love will flourish as judgment is replaced by understanding and compassion. We are on the threshold of a revolutionary transformation of spirituality.

"I can tell you the meaning of the truth, although you also have to understand it for yourself. The truth is that we are God. It is as simple as that. That is the only truth we need to grasp. Note that it is not important if we grasp this truth in this lifetime. We can always do it in another." Peter stepped back.

"Next question?" I asked, nodding toward the line.

A middle-aged, bearded man said, "You guys sound so serious and believing. What makes you so sure that we are one with God?"

I answered this one. "Don't accept our word for it. Find out for yourself. Personally, we both believe it. In fact, we think we *know* it. We've both come to this conclusion through personal experiences, and that should be your method as well. This is why Peter said earlier that you need to come to your *own* beliefs, and that we don't want people to accept our beliefs as dogma. Spirituality is your responsibility, and not mine to give you. That being said, I still think I *know*.

"It's difficult to explain in words, because I came to my realization through personal experience. I can't tell you what to read or what to do to find God. For me, it was a combination of experiences and exposures – reading, listening, seeing. After a period of time, it was as if a light

Chapter Three - Los Angeles Lecture

went on in my mind. I suddenly *knew*. It was subtle in its manifestation. Over time, however, it became a powerful feeling of *knowing*. Today, I have no doubt of my divinity, and it gives me incredible peace of mind.

"I'm not the only one who *knows*," I continued. "Every day, more and more people are becoming Gnostic and have a direct connection with God. I think it is wonderful that people are becoming aware of their oneness with God. It is creating a shift in society and is leading to something extraordinary, something of biblical proportions.

"The impact of this new spiritual awareness will replace our current way of life. These are revolutionary ideas that impact how society is formulated. However, I'm not afraid to be a revolutionary if it is going to lead to something better. I think George Washington was a revolutionary for the same reason. However, I'm not going to fight with guns, only ideas," I added jokingly.

I paused. "Next question?"

A lady in her thirties came up to the microphone. She had short blonde hair and blue eyes. "To follow up on what you just said, if people begin to believe that we are all one, won't existing social institutions collapse?"

"It's going to be the other way around," I replied. "First, our institutions will collapse, and *then* we will question our beliefs. Once we begin to reorganize society, new beliefs will begin to take hold. The belief in oneness will be at the forefront of those new beliefs.

"If you left today to go live in space, and then came back in 2050, you'd be in awe at the change that had transpired while you were gone. *Everything* will change. Our social, political, cultural, and economic systems will transform. A new civilization will have arisen."

A lady with long, curly red hair approached the aisle microphone. "Will this change be traumatic? Will there be violence?"

I looked at Peter. He approached the lectern. "The energy vibration on the planet is increasing, thereby diminishing the threat of violence. For this reason, I do not think the transition will be extremely violent or include a civil war. However, I am not sure how violence can be avoided. I expect riots in the major cities, and I would not recommend living in the major metropolitan areas for too many more years. Smaller communities will be much safer and relatively peaceful as love begins to flourish.

"Understand, the economy will slow down, and that is going to have huge implications. So, yes, it will be traumatic. The current civilization is based on materialism and growth. When these ideals fail, we will experience trauma on a large scale. The effects are going to be widely felt.

"The outcome will be new communities that will arise out of nowhere. These new communities will be created for survival and will not be thriving hubs of economic activity. Instead, they will focus on sustainability and simplicity.

"As you can imagine, the transition will not be easy. Our standard of living will fall dramatically over the next few decades. Technologically, we will stagnate for a period of time, and then it will proliferate. From then on, the planet will be highly technological, much more so than today. Although, before you get too excited about civilization's optimistic future, realize that the population will be much smaller, less than 20 percent of its current size. Thus, a lot of lives are going to be lost during this transition. It is not going to be easy.

"I would like to make one more point before we leave," Peter continued. "Many of you may be depressed with all

Chapter Three - Los Angeles Lecture

this talk of lost lives and trauma. But I submit that it is a time to be joyous. We are looking at the birth of a new civilization and the death of an outdated one. Yes, there will be pain and suffering during the transition. But look at the result. We will have a planet based on truth, where love thrives. This is something to anticipate, and we should be grateful for our front-row seat. Believe me, we are lucky to be here to experience this event."

I approached the lectern. "Thank you for coming. You can order an MP3 file or CD of the lecture at the back of the room. Also, there are books and CDs for sale. If you want to order on the Internet, you can use my web page. If anyone has a book they would like me to sign, I will be up here in front. Thank you again for coming."

The crowd rose and headed for the exits. Several people approached Peter and me with questions, which we answered for another twenty minutes. And I signed several copies of my books. Finally, we were done and went back to our hotel.

Chapter Four

Trip to San Francisco

After the lecture, Peter and I went back to our hotel suite to change into something more casual for our drive to San Francisco. While walking to the room, I asked Peter if he wanted to take a side trip.

"I have a friend in L.A. that we should visit. She lives in Santa Monica, which is on the way. I'll call her and see if she's home."

"Okay," Peter said.

After we changed, I called Julie from the room, and she invited us to come over. "Let's go," I said to Peter, hanging up the phone. "She's expecting us."

We checked out of the hotel and headed for Santa Monica. The sun was shining, and it was a typical 80-degree day in Southern California. We drove on the 405 freeway, with the windows down and smiles on our faces. Both of us were having a great time.

"You'll like Julie," I said. "She's an Aquarian-bohemian, New Age hippie. She's very smart and a devoted lightworker. Her house is filled with crystals, incense, angels, and other New Age decorations. You'll get an idea about her when we walk into her house. I met Julie a few years ago at a Peggy Phoenix Dubro seminar on energy healing."

I didn't tell Peter that Julie was thirty, single, and beautiful. I decided to see if she made his heart flutter, as mine always did in her presence. A man had to be dead inside not to feel something around her.

Julie lived a few blocks from the ocean, in an old house built in the 1950s. I saw her yellow Volkswagen Beetle parked in the driveway. I parked in front, and we walked to the house.

With a big smile, Julie opened the front door. Her short dark hair, blue eyes, and lithe body captivated us.

I lunged forward and hugged her tightly. "Hi," I said.

"Who is this, John?" she asked, with piqued interest.

"Julie, meet Peter. He's lecturing with me on the tour."

She shook Peter's hand and said hello.

I couldn't tell if Peter's heart was fluttering, but he definitely was glad we came. He smiled at Julie. "It is a pleasure to meet you. Would you like to come to San Francisco with us?"

Julie looked at me. "John? Where did that come from?"

I smiled and shrugged. "Why not? What are you doing this weekend?"

She laughed. "Nothing. Let's see. Today is Saturday.... I guess I could fly back Sunday night. You're going to Seattle next, right? Are you driving to San Francisco today?"

I nodded. "Yeah. Let's go in and talk about it."

We went inside, and indeed I could smell incense. A soothing Robert Coxon CD was playing on her stereo. Several prints of angels decorated the walls. *The Sedona Journal of Emergence* magazine lay on the coffee table. A large white-marble angel filled one of the corners. A bookshelf with an array of crystals was in another corner. We each found a place to sit.

"We planned to visit with you for an hour or so," I said to Julie, "and then head to San Francisco. But Peter took one

Chapter Four – Trip to San Francisco

look at you and wanted *two* days." I laughed, and so did they.

"I suppose that is true," Peter said. "Actually, I asked her because I thought she might like to come."

"Okay," Julie said. "I'm coming. Let me pack, and we'll be on our way. I have to call a friend to watch my dog, but that will only take a minute." She headed for her bedroom to pack.

This trip was actually getting better, I thought. If you travel with a three-thousand-year-old man, I suppose you're bound to find some magic along the way.

After Julie packed and made her phone call, we piled into my car and were on our way.

"So, are you still giving your doom and gloom speech, John?" Julie asked as I drove.

"Yes, and you'd better begin planning to leave L.A. I'm planning to move to Colorado soon, and you should decide where you want to live."

In her best cynical voice, Julie said, "John, you've been telling me for years that the economy is going to collapse. When is this big crash going to occur?"

"Sooner than you think," Peter said from the back seat.

Julie turned to look at Peter. "So, you believe in this impending collapse, too? I don't, and I'm not leaving Santa Monica. I love it here, next to the ocean."

"Peter, we have to tell her," I said. "You said to keep it a secret, but I think this is a situation where we can make an exception."

"Okay," he said.

"What are you guys talking about?" Julie asked.

"Peter will tell you."

Julie turned to Peter.

"I have been waiting thousands of years for what is about to occur," Peter said. "I am an *immortal*. I have been alive for three thousand years on this planet, and I do not age. You may think this is impossible, but it is true. Recently, I came to the United States to experience the transition that is fast approaching. It will begin soon, and John is correct in warning you to begin planning your exit from Los Angeles. The chaos is going to be unbearable in large metro cities."

Julie stared at Peter. "You're an immortal?" She said skeptically. "Is there any way you can prove it?"

"Sure. We need a plastic bag. John, stop at the next store, so we can get one."

"Why?" Julie said incredulously. "Are you going to suffocate yourself?"

Peter nodded. "After I stop breathing, take the bag off my head and check my pulse. Within minutes, my heart will start beating, and I will begin breathing."

"This is too weird," Julie said, shaking her head. "What if you don't start breathing? What would we do then? Tell the cops that we watched you kill yourself? Oh, well, he told us he was an immortal."

Everyone laughed.

Peter looked at me, trying hard not to laugh. "John, do you trust me?"

I looked at Julie. "Let's do it, if it will convince you."

"Is there any other way that you can convince me?" Julie asked Peter.

"Do you know any psychics in San Francisco that you trust? They could confirm my age. But the bag *will* work. I have done it a few times. There will not be a problem. I learned about it when someone tried to suffocate me in the twelfth century in Southern France during the Albigensian

Chapter Four – Trip to San Francisco

Crusade. I tried to help save the Cathars, but I failed." Peter said.

Peter and I waited for Julie to reply.

"Okay, let's get the bag," she said.

I pulled off Interstate 5 in Santa Clarita, one of the various suburban cities outside Los Angeles, and found a store that carried plastic bags. Minutes later, we parked on a secluded road.

Peter sat in the back seat and put a plastic bag over his head, then tied it around his neck himself. Within a minute, he stopped breathing, and his body went limp.

"Check his pulse," I said to Julie.

"His heart stopped!" she exclaimed, suddenly looking terrified.

I untied the bag and removed it from his head. Julie and I waited, but Julie began to panic. "My God, this is crazy!" she screamed.

"Relax," I said calmly. "He'll start breathing again. Let's just wait patiently."

I was confident that Peter would begin breathing again. Sure enough, minutes later his chest started expanding and contracting.

"He's breathing!" Julie exclaimed, with heartfelt relief.

I smiled.

She looked at me. "You knew."

"I was pretty confident."

Soon, Peter's eyes opened, and it was as if nothing had happened. "Let's get going," he said.

"Wow!" Julie said. "I can't believe what just happened."

"Wait until the transition begins," Peter said. "You will be saying 'wow' more often than you can imagine. The world is getting ready to metaphorically turn upside down."

"Now I'm interested," Julie said to Peter. "What is going to happen and why?"

"Well, I am glad we have your attention," he said. "You are going to be very helpful once the transition begins. You will not be afraid now. Instead, you will be helping others to understand."

"I know," Julie replied cynically. "I've been to the seminars and lectures. I know that we lightworkers are here to help the coming shift. So, what's going to happen?"

"No one knows exactly *how* or *what* will transpire. People such as John and I have an idea, or vision, of what will happen. We know the themes that will have major impacts. For instance, love will slowly and steadily replace power as the foundation of civilization. It won't happen overnight and will require four generations to culminate. But it will become palpable by 2035, and noticeably by 2030, that this change is underway."

Peter paused, then continued.

"That is not going to happen easily. Currently, power is the basis for the economy, politics, and even social institutions. How could we possibly transform these foundations of humanity without major upheaval? That is why John has been talking about societal collapse and its likely outcome." Peter paused and waited for Julie to reply.

"My initial response," she said, "is that I find it implausible that love will be the basis of society. It sounds too utopian. Men have always coveted power. I can't even imagine human behavior changing that drastically."

"I can understand that reaction," Peter said. "As a lightworker, however, you should understand that subtle energy affects us all. The planet is currently changing from being mired in negative dark energy, to positive light energy. This energy shift will usher in an age of love. Why

Chapter Four - Trip to San Francisco

is this happening? My answer is that it has been planned for millennia...."

"By whom?" Julie interrupted.

"The answer, of course, is God," Peter replied. "Nothing is haphazard in the universe. God is in complete control. This transformation of humanity is going to initiate fairly quickly. By 2050, the change will be so dramatic that humanity will not resemble today, although there will be many conscientious objectors – mostly nihilists and fundamentalist Christians – to the revolution that is underway. We will go from a focus on power to a focus on love in one generation."

"Okay, I'm starting to understand," Julie said sincerely. "The New Age is almost here, and the transition period will be very chaotic, but short. Both of you are informing others in the hope that they will understand and help. I get it. But why will Santa Monica be threatened? Why can't I stay here?"

"Because," Peter said, "Los Angeles will most likely be one of the worst places to live. There will be social chaos, crime, violence, and perhaps some earthquakes. There will be too many people and not enough resources. The Los Angeles basin is already one of the most violent places in the country. Someone is murdered here every day. There are over one hundred thousand armed gang members living here. These gangs are at war right now. What's going to happen when social chaos unfolds? I am not optimistic about your neighborhood.

"Eventually, you will leave, but it is better to leave in an orderly manner. For instance, your house will likely be worth half its value in a few years. Why not sell it now, while it has value? Why take the risk? The major cities will be much more turbulent than small communities. People, especially in California, will be thinking, wondering, where to go? We are telling you to begin planning because it is time to get ready."

Julie laughed. "Every time I try to believe you, you make another incredible statement. My house will be half its value in a few years? How can that happen? Everyone wants to live in Santa Monica, two blocks from the ocean."

"Today, but not in a few years," I said. "Soon, people will be leaving Los Angeles en masse. There will be so many abandoned homes that no one will have to pay to own one."

"Wow, you guys really believe this?"

"Let me get back to my answer," Peter said. "The end of the current civilization is very near. There have been plans and decisions made. This planet will soon have a new civilization. And the plan is for a relatively swift transition, with the majority of the changes occurring within one generation. So, once it starts, you don't want to be in the wrong place."

"Okay, I'll think about moving," Julie said.

Peter smiled. "The future may initially be chaotic, but it's really the pain of giving birth to a new civilization. Peace is not very far away. Whereas the last two thousand years have been primarily bloody and patriarchal, the next civilization will be peaceful and equitable. Women and men will be treated as equals, as will each race. No longer will race relations or religious affiliations separate people and splinter our culture. People will learn to get along. Yes, it is a utopian dream, but it is near, and it will be a reality.

"In many ways, Julie," Peter continued, "the New Age will be boring. The negative energy that currently envelops this planet creates incredible opportunities to experience all aspects of life. That makes life exciting. Look at the way people treat each other now. In Los Angeles, you can be threatened, hated, robbed, harassed, and intimidated, all

Chapter Four - Trip to San Francisco

in the same week. The array of negative opportunities is endless. This will all change when love replaces power, and spiritual awareness envelops the planet. In the near future, people will experience only harmony and joy. Like I said, life will be boring, compared to the way it is today. The array of experiences will diminish significantly."

"Peace and harmony?" Julie said. "It sounds okay to me, but I'm still skeptical. Keep talking, though. I'm listening."

Peter continued. "Once we advance spiritually, we begin to prefer boring. Instead of excitement, we decide that we like peace and harmony. As the transition begins, this preference will begin to manifest. However, not everyone is going to accept this change easily. Young souls, those who currently hold most of the power in society, prefer excitement and stimulation. This is one of the reasons the transition will be so traumatic. Young souls abhor peace and harmony. They intuitively understand that they need a power-based culture where they can find opportunities to stand out as individuals. Peace and harmony bring people together into homogenous groups, which are repulsive to young souls. Why? Because it emasculates their power, which is something young-soul alpha males abhor.

"America currently is comprised of approximately 35 percent young souls. This creates a looming problem for the transition. Young souls currently control nearly everything. They are the 5 percent who have 90 percent of the wealth. By their nature, they seek achievement. They are the politicians and leaders of industry. They are the current power structure. And they will not be cooperative with old and mature souls who understand the nature of the transition, which is one of harmony and compassion.

"Mature and old souls will both welcome the transition, knowing that this is the only way forward for humanity.

That it is our only choice. Mature souls are concerned with emotions and prefer relationships with people versus achievement. Old souls are concerned for the betterment of humanity and have little desire to achieve for themselves. Although many mature and old souls are achievers, they have different reasons for achieving, and would easily drop their achievements for a culture based on love and compassion.

"Young souls, on the other hand, achieve for themselves and would not easily give up their positions of power. They believe that peace and harmony are merely a pipe dream, and the least of their concerns. They believe that human nature requires a class-bassed society, with achievers on top, and stragglers on the bottom.

"This also will be true of the military, intelligence agencies, and government. They will perceive the transition as a period of turmoil that they must control and overcome. In the beginning, they will do everything they can to control the events, and this will slow the transition during the first few years.

"We, the lightworkers must bide our time and communicate to the world what we know. The first decade of the transition is about communication and spreading the word. Aquarius is an air sign and is ideal for communicating. Aquarius is the water bearer, which is analogous to an outpouring of information to benefit all of humanity. The Internet will be very helpful for this outpouring of information. It fits in perfectly with the Age of Aquarius.

"Initially, there will be too much resistance from young souls for lightworkers to have a dramatic influence on society. All we can do is spread the word and create small spiritual communities. In time, the young souls will lose their power as the economy declines and social institutions

Chapter Four - Trip to San Francisco

implode. The initial resistance to transformational change will last about a decade. After that, the old souls, particularly women, will begin to assume control."

"How can that happen? Old soul, women will assume control?" Julie asked skeptically, turning and looking at Peter in the back seat.

Peter looked at Julie. "It does sound crazy, doesn't it? The trigger will be when the truth begins being released to society by mainstream outlets, such as Netflix and YouTube. The truth can no longer be held at bay. It wants to come out, and it will."

"What truth," Julie asked, still looking at Peter.

"That there is only one consciousness which we all share."

"Suddenly, society is going to believe in non-duality?" Julie asked skeptically.

Peter nodded. "Yes, enough will believe to create a paradigm shift. Not everyone will believe, but enough to begin a trend toward creating a new society based on that idea. The idea that we are all one, so let's create a society based on harmony, where we live in peace."

"And we can we expect peace in the near future?" Julie asked, turning back around.

"It depends on your perspective," Peter said. "From a young soul's viewpoint, the world will be chaotic, mired in economic malaise. In some respects, they will be correct. There will be shortages of food, water, and energy. Jobs will be scarce, if not impossible to find. People will die by the millions from disease. Many will wonder if it is ever going to get better.

"However, many will know that it is indeed going to get better and that we are literally living through the birth pains of a new civilization that is rising. These will be the new leaders. They will have vision and spiritual wisdom. They will be the lightworkers, like John and myself. We *know* that it is going to get better. It is simply a matter of allowing it to happen. Of course, the key is understanding objective truth."

"Objective truth? What is that?" Julie exclaimed.

"Truth is always true. This axiom will be the foundation of the next civilization. All lies will fade away in significance, and the truth shall reign. The most fundamental of these truths is that we are God. That our core self, which is our soul, is connected to God. That there is no separation between us and God, or between us and anything. Thus, we are eternal, with this life being just a blip of reincarnational experience. And that this single lifetime has very little impact on the overall makeup of our soul. This lifetime is not as serious as we make it out to be. It's just one lifetime for an eternal soul."

"Wow," she said with a sense of wonder. "*That* is where this civilization is going? That type of understanding of reality?"

"Yes. Spiritually, this planet will be making a quantum leap in spiritual awareness, and it will be this generation that not only puts it in motion, but many will have a huge spiritual awakening. In fact, many will ascend to the New Earth in the 5th dimension. That's where I'm planning to go."

As I drove north through the San Joaquin Valley on Interstate 5, I observed the various farm crops as I listened intently to the conversation.

"Peter," Julie said, "you seem to be implying that there is not a lot of meaning to this lifetime. What do you mean by, 'our current lifetime has little impact on the soul?'"

"Overall impact," he said. "One lifetime spent on a planet is just a blip of experience to an immortal soul. The

Chapter Four - Trip to San Francisco

current belief in only one lifetime will soon be superseded by the new dominant belief that we are all God and have lived many lifetimes."

Julie nodded. "That would be nice, but then what? Where does that leave the meaning of life? How do we construct society around that belief?"

"Life has meaning simply because it exists," Peter said. "In other words, life itself is the meaning, although the evolution of the soul does play a part. This answer may sound cryptic, but it is a profound question with no easy answer. To think that our lives have meaning, or that we can create a more meaningful life, is an illusion. Each person's life cannot be compared to another's. In other words, no life is more meaningful than another."

Peter continued on. "If you want to define the meaning of life as the evolution of the soul, then that is fine. That can be your definition. In fact, each person can have their own definition. However, for society to have a definition, that would be limiting, and not the whole truth. As I said before, life itself is the meaning.

"The 'meaning of life' has no single answer. Each individual must have their own beliefs and come to their own conclusions. These are things that cannot be written or explained. They are unique for each of us."

"Then what do we use as the basis for society?" Julie asked.

"Humanity," Peter replied. "That will be the underlying consideration: what is best for humanity? Underlying that concept of humanity is equity and treating everyone as equals. Instead of using religious dogma for our values, we will use the sustainability of humanity, and the planet itself as our highest values. Religion and spirituality will be an individual matter. Within a few generations, all religious institutions will be historical relics."

"I like that," Julie replied enthusiastically. "Basically, you're saying that each individual will have their own religion. What about society as a whole? Won't we share common beliefs?"

Peter nodded. "We will become aware of our connectedness. We will come to see ourselves in others, literally mirrors of each other. We will come to realize that there are only two entities: ourselves, and everything else. And that we all share the mind of God."

I smiled at Peter through the rearview mirror to acknowledge that I understood him. Then I looked at Julie, next to me in the front seat. "Do you understand?"

"Well, not exactly," she said. "How can we share the mind of God, when we each have our own?"

"Yes, we each have our own," I said, "but we all share a larger mind, the mind of God. The intelligence of the soul encompasses more than just our brain, much more. The mind of God integrates us into one. For example, as each cell in our body is in contact with our brain, each soul is in contact with the larger mind of God. Everyone is connected, just like the cells in our bodies."

I smiled. "We are literally cells in the body of God. And, as each cell is equivalent, so are souls. From God's standpoint, souls are souls. Just as from our standpoint, cells are cells. We cherish our cells equally. We can't tell one red blood cell from another. This is only an analogy, but it gives you an idea of how we are related."

"Interesting," Julie said. "So, you're saying that there is a greater mind, which is the mind of God, and that our soul is part of that mind. We think we are separate, but the separateness is an illusion."

Chapter Four – Trip to San Francisco

"Exactly," I said.

"So, the truth," Peter added from the back seat, "is that we are all part of God, and eternal. And because we are God, and God is eternal, we are eternal. God created us to experience the infinite, and to be creators with our own free will. However, on our journey, we have to learn to create responsibly. This current lifetime that we are experiencing is about learning to create responsibly. This explanation is simplified, but you get the idea. We are all here to learn."

Julie looked back at Peter. "We're all little, immortal gods, huh? And we all have creator abilities?"

Peter nodded.

"That's a bit of a leap from the human fragileness that I currently feel," Julie said.

"You need to have more sex," Peter said. "That will give you more self-confidence and make you feel like an immortal god."

We all laughed.

"So, that's what you learned in 3,000 years?" Julie asked.

We laughed more.

* * * * *

We arrived in San Francisco late in the afternoon. Julie recommended that we go to Golden Gate Park and have a picnic. We found a deli and bought sandwiches, fruit, and something to drink. We were all in good spirits.

We arrived at the park feeling exuberant. The sun was shining, and the park was beautiful. There were flowers, trimmed hedges, and acres of cut green grass. I was with good friends and didn't have a worry in my mind. All I wanted to do was enjoy the day.

We walked barefoot on the grass and looked for a place to sit under a tree, out of the sun. After a short stroll, we found a place, somewhat isolated, which provided solace and shade. The homeless people were scattered throughout the park, and it was easy to surmise that this was home for many of them.

"Peter," I said, "is the homeless problem in the U.S. today different from the poverty of the past, or is it the same?"

"Much different," he said. "The numbers are about the same, about 1 percent of the population, but the makeup is entirely different. Today, you have homeless people with incredible abilities. I remember a story about a homeless man who was truly brilliant and well-read. He had lost his job and did not have any savings. Without any family or friends, his only recourse was the streets. After a week on the streets, he was so frustrated with trying to get help that he gave up and decided to be homeless as a protestor. More precisely, he decided to be a martyr. He was so angry that someone with abilities could fall through the cracks that he quit looking for work. That would never have occurred in the past. Today, you have educated people who find themselves homeless, people you would consider 'normal,' if only they had not taken a wrong turn or lost their job.

"This fact," Peter continued, "has created an untenable situation. America has serious social problems that will bring it down, and in fact, are bringing it down. The homeless problem is indicative of other, more serious, social problems. America is not taking care of its own. America takes care of the elderly, the disabled, and many veterans, but has ignored the downtrodden. Worse, America has stigmatized them and blamed them for their problems.

Chapter Four - Trip to San Francisco

"You cannot mock God, and that is what is happening in America. I will tell you why the homeless problem is mocking God. Not because, as a society, we have homelessness. That is not the problem, because some people will choose that experience. The problem is with society mocking those who are homeless. Do you see the distinction? Homelessness is okay. Mocking those who are homeless is not.

"In the past, when people became homeless, they did not hold a grudge against society; they accepted their fate and then tried to move their lives forward. Likewise, those who were not homeless were quick to lend a helping hand or a bowl of soup. Today, millions of people are impoverished and feel they should not be. They feel lurking eyes from people judging them as unworthy. From this feeling, they hold a grudge, and they are angry.

"In America today, the impoverished are angrier about their fate than in the past. Indeed, they feel their pain much more acutely. They feel society's judging eyes."

"All I know," Julie said, "is that too many people are homeless. We have created a civilization in which people must fend for themselves in a competitive battle of the fittest. It's a competition of winners and losers, and if someone ends up homeless, then they are the losers. There is something humanely deficient in an affluent society that allows homelessness to be so pervasive."

"Yes," Peter said, "you are correct. America is allowing something that is humanely deficient. That is where God comes in and makes changes. God hears our collective groans of frustration. And God will respond in kind. This is why society is going to change. Humanity wants a better way to live."

"People are vocal about programs for the elderly, such as Medicare and Social Security," I added, "yet they are blasé, and even antagonistic, toward programs for the poor. This society is screwed up, and not enough people care. All we hear about is the greatness of this country. If we even mention poverty problems, people respond with hostility against socialism. They'll tell us to go live in another country and see how we like it there."

"A large segment of Americans is affluent," Peter said. "These mostly young souls are having such a good time making and spending money that they do not have time to fret over those who are left behind. After all, young souls do not have a conscience. As far as they are concerned, life is a contest. To the victor go the spoils.

"What we need is a Spiritual Bill of Rights.[2] It would not need to be a legal document, just something that can be used for guidance. It could include the following:

All Beings are created equal and possess the same qualities as their Creator.

All Beings have the right to joy, laughter, and Love.

All Beings are granted full freedom as their Spirit directs them, without interference, manipulation, or judgment from another Being.

All Beings are entitled to all resources that are required to maintain Life in Physicality, without respect to their personal beliefs, behaviors, or actions.

All Beings may disagree with any other Beings without fear of intimidation, retribution, imprisonment, torture, or death.

All Beings recognize that all forms of legal governance are imperfect and temporary, and that the ultimate Divine Authority resides within each Being.

All Expressions of the Creator are deemed living Beings – whether animal, mineral, or plant – and are accorded the rights previously stated."

Chapter Four - Trip to San Francisco

"Where did you learn that?" Julie asked.

"These concepts were channeled from St. Germain, an Ascended Master."

"That's beautiful," Julie replied. "The world would be such a better place if we used those ideas."

"It will not be long before we begin using them," Peter said. "You can mock God only so much before the tide of change awakens. We are close to the breaking point. I can already hear the cracks."

Peter smiled and stretched his toes so that they made a cracking sound. Julie and I laughed at his immortal body sounds. We stopped talking to eat and were quiet for several minutes, just reflecting and enjoying the day. Julie finally broke the silence.

"Let's change the subject," Julie said. "Peter, what about relationships between men and women? How have they changed over the centuries?"

"There are differences are dramatic, especially here in America. It has been fascinating to behold. In the past, women were literally slaves. They had no rights, legal or social. They had their place, and it was decidedly determined by men. Because men had such a one-sided domination over women, it was inevitable that this relationship would evolve. It has, and it continues to evolve. Many women, like yourself, take your equality with men for granted. Other women throughout the world still struggle with it every day. And it really has not been that long since women did not have any rights in society. Many of the advances for women came in the last one hundred years, mostly in America. Before that, women were basically powerless.

"The Middle East today is a good example of this powerlessness," Peter continued. "Women in parts of the Middle East are considered owned by men. In some countries, women cannot sign legal documents, have a bank account, drive a car, or even travel without a male companion. That is how it has always been for most women until just the last few generations.

"With that historical perspective," Peter added, "look at the relationships in America today. They are incredible! For the first time in this civilization's history, men and women have the opportunity to share their lives on an equal footing. They can view each other as equals. Men today are cooking and cleaning for their families; women are earning income to pay the bills. Roles are reversing and intermixing. It is a beautiful experience. This social evolution is the most wonderful thing I have witnessed.

"On the downside, it is new, and some people are having trouble adapting to the new reality. Men are hanging onto their traditional roles, and women are confused about what roles to play. Thus, many relationships today are emotionally trying. People are having a difficult time finding the right balance in relationships. But I do not see all this as negative. I see it more as an opportunity to learn about equality.

"The beautiful thing," Peter continued, "is that people have the opportunity to share their lives on an equal footing. You do not know how long people have yearned for this. I have witnessed relationships for thousands of years, and nothing compares to the relationships that exist today. In the past, men were always on a pedestal and held the power. Thus, men and women could not share equality on a social level. In essence, men were forced to marry virtual slaves, where women were expected to do as they were told. Even today in modern Japan, women often walk behind their husbands."

Peter looked at Julie. "Do you comprehend the significance of relationships today versus the past? No longer

Chapter Four - Trip to San Francisco

are women considered inferior by society. Only one hundred years ago, women could not vote in this country. The degree of change that has occurred is monumental. No longer are men marrying women whose hands are tied, metaphorically, behind their backs. Today, and more so as each day passes, women are being viewed on equal terms with men. This development allows men and women to love each other on a level that was not possible until only recently.

"Interestingly, it has been American women who have been the trailblazers. Your generation, Julie, has been instrumental in forcing civilization to acknowledge women. Your example will free the women of the Middle East and everywhere else on this planet. Denying women equality can only last for another decade or two."

Peter waited for Julie to reply.

"God can only be mocked so much?" Julie asked rhetorically.

"Exactly," Peter smiled. "Women of the world are uniting in their quest for equality. It is inevitable. And God's hand is at work. Do not forget, this is God's world. We create the mess, but God cleans it up. Well, we clean it up together, because we are God.

Julie smiled. "I wish God would clean up my mess. I can't seem to have a relationship that doesn't result in chaos and heartache."

There was an uncomfortable period of silence as we contemplated how personal this conversation could get.

"Maybe I can help," Peter finally said. "Your biggest problem is most likely communication. Do you say what is on your mind? Or do you keep your thoughts to yourself? Are you open or secretive in your relationships?"

Julie contemplated. "I see what you're getting at, and you're right. I always find myself afraid to say what's on my mind. I feel like it will lead to tension or a fight if I say what I'm thinking. Yeah, I always have trouble communicating. Eventually, I feel like we have different desires, and that's when I leave."

Peter smiled. "You are courageous to leave. Most women do not leave and are stuck in relationships that are not harmonious. Try this next time. Begin your relationship with open, honest communication. Tell the other person what you want out of the relationship. Tell him your ideas about how relationships should work. Tell him everything about yourself. Tell him what is important to you and how you want to live your life. Tell him your needs and fears. Be brutally honest. Open up completely and let him know who you are and what drives you. That's communication.

"If you do not communicate completely in the beginning, the details left unsaid can destroy the relationship. Honesty and communication are the keys to relationships. Not sex, money, or even love."

Julie looked confused. "Not love? What do you mean?"

"Well, true love is rare. And most relationships exist on a boring level of communication and sharing your lives. If you do experience true love, you can overcome any adversity, even a lack of communication. Then you are in a relationship that does not have any serious problems. True love is so powerful that you relish every moment. You cannot bear to be apart.

"For those not blessed with true love, communication is paramount, and dissolution of the relationship is always a possibility. For those who find true love, dissolution is not a possibility. Those fortunate souls would rather die than be separated. The rest of us must rely on honesty and communication."

Chapter Four - Trip to San Francisco

Peter paused and looked at Julie. "You might find true love in this lifetime, but the odds are actually small. Instead, most of us are faced with learning how to communicate with a partner. Thus, sex, money, and love are secondary to communication for creating a happy relationship. Now, if communication is so important, why does society place so much emphasis on sex, money, and love? The answer is an emphasis on the lower chakras, which express the energies that currently dominate society. This will soon change, and relationships will become much better. We will begin to focus more on the heart chakra.

"Today, instead of communicating, most couples create agreed roles and act as if those roles are normal. Then they do not talk about the roles they assume. The result is the trap that you constantly find yourself in; playing a fictitious role that you no longer like. That is why it is so important to communicate at the beginning of a relationship. If you state the things that you like to do and get acknowledgment from your partner that he or she will allow you to experience those things, then you can do them. Do you see how powerful communication can be? Once you learn to communicate with each other, changes in a relationship become much easier. It can help you from getting trapped in a role that you don't like.

"I know of relationships that are so communicative that the couple can live separately for months without any problem. Todd, a friend of mine in Ireland, and his wife, Ursula, love their freedom and individuality. She constantly travels without him. He accepts this as part of their relationship. Ursula will stay home for months, and then suddenly say she is going to France. Todd will smile and say, 'See you when you get back.' They communicate their needs and allow each other the freedom to fulfill those needs.

"It is not a shock to Todd when Ursula needs to get out of the house without him. She communicates to him this need of hers. Likewise, he acknowledges to her that he will allow her these experiences. This is only one example, but you get the idea of the importance of communication."

Julie smiled. "I want to have a relationship like that!"

I wanted to say something like, "We could try," but I kept my mouth shut and listened to the conversation.

"You can," Peter replied. "Just make sure that you continue to tell each other your needs and fears. Do not make it a one-time conversation at the beginning of the relationship. I remember watching the movie *Heat* with Al Pacino. His wife was frustrated because he would not communicate with her. I remember one scene where he tells her that he has to remain sharp and snaps his fingers a few times. It was his excuse for not talking to her. They loved each other, but that was not enough for her. She was desperately frustrated that the relationship was not what she wanted, but it was too late to change it. She did not communicate her needs *before* they got married. Now she was stuck in a relationship where communication was not possible."

* * * * *

We finished lunch and left the park. Then we found three hotel rooms for the night. By then, the sun was setting, yet it was still warm outside. We decided to walk from the hotel to Fisherman's Wharf, a few blocks away, to find a restaurant for dinner. Afterward, we found a coffee bar and talked. It was a very enjoyable evening.

The next day, Sunday morning, we took a ride to Stinson Beach in Marin County to see Dr. Glenn, a friend of mine.

Chapter Four - Trip to San Francisco

I had called him Saturday night and asked if he would be home, and he invited us over.

When we arrived, we went straight to the beach. Fog obscured the sun, but we didn't mind. The three of us walked on the beach for an hour, enjoying the exercise, ocean air, and each other's company. The trip was turning into a memorable experience for all of us. Peter and I both were flirting with Julie. I had been in love with her since I first met her. Now I think Peter was smitten as well.

After walking on the beach, we went to Dr. Glenn's house, a couple of blocks away. I will always remember the time he let me and a friend borrow his car to visit San Francisco. I won't go into details, but I still owe him a favor for the fantastic time we had.

As the three of us approached the front door, it opened, and Dr. Glenn was there to greet us.

"Dr. Glenn, hi, it's good to see you," I said, as we shook hands. I squeezed hard to prevent my fingers from being injured; he had large hands and a strong grip. Dr. Glenn was a big, burly man with an easy smile, intense eyes, and a large, white beard. "I brought two friends you will enjoy meeting. This is Peter, a friend from Europe, and Julie, a long-time friend from Santa Monica."

Dr. Glenn smiled and shook hands with Peter and Julie. "Hello, please come inside." He turned, and we followed him into the living room. A fire burned in the fireplace and the room was warm. A cat was curled up in a chair, asleep next to the fire. The room was cozy. It reminded me of a log cabin, with its wooden walls, brown carpet, and dark brown sofas.

"Please have a seat," Dr. Glenn said to us. "Is there anything I can get you? Coffee, tea, water, orange juice?"

"What are you drinking?" Julie asked him.

Dr. Glenn smiled. "Coffee. Will you join me?"

"Please," she said. "Black."

He looked at Peter, then me. We both said we were fine.

We made ourselves comfortable and waited for Dr. Glenn to return with Julie's coffee.

"John," he said, when he returned, "every time you come and see me, I hear stories of the end of the world. Yet, here we are."

Julie laughed. "You, too? If you hang out with these two, you would think the sky is falling."

I smiled. "I've been telling Dr. Glenn for years that a societal breakdown is coming. He gives me a bad time because I don't have an exact date when these events will start occurring."

Peter turned to Dr. Glenn. "I can't give you a date, either. The best I can do is predict that a serious economic downturn will begin soon, which will quickly lead to an economic malaise. How soon? Imminent is my guess. Once this downturn begins, this country will begin a spiral of deterioration, leading to the breakup of the United States."

Dr. Glenn raised his eyebrows. "Imminent. That's a strong word."

"Indeed," Peter replied. "There will be a few signs that precede the economic crisis. The first thing to look for is an explosion in debt, as both the U.S. government and the Fed add debt to their balance sheets. This will begin to weaken the dollar, which will cause gold and silver to surge, as investors seek a safe haven. These will be the precursors for a stock market crash. Then you will see bailouts and more money printing by the Federal Reserve. However, this will only further destabilize the economy because of inflation, eventually leading to the insolvency of the financial system,

Chapter Four – Trip to San Francisco

the default of government bonds, and the bankruptcy of the United States."

"You give a harsh view," Dr. Glenn said lightly. His doubts were obvious, despite his good-natured tone.

Peter stared intently at Dr. Glenn. "That is only the beginning. Once the economy falters, we are going to see shortages in everything: gasoline, diesel electricity, food, water, toilet paper, you name it. Nothing will be in abundance, except hardship. It is going to be a difficult period."

"Food shortages in America?" Dr. Glenn said skeptically. "That's a stretch. We export 50 percent of our wheat. I think we can feed ourselves."

"Indeed, we won't starve," Peter replied. "But prices will increase, and shortages of common items will become common. For many communities, food will be grown and eaten locally. Energy shortages are going to make it difficult to grow and transport food economically. Also, the economic infrastructure is going to collapse, removing important market factions. In fact, over a short period of time, the corporation as we know it today, will disappear. There will no longer be McDonald's, Taco Bell, Safeway, or Walgreens."

Dr. Glenn raised his eyebrows. "You sound more convincing than John. I don't hear any doubt in your voice at all. Should I be nervous?"

With a smile, I said, "You don't have to go anywhere, Dr. Glenn. Stinson Beach is tucked away up here. You have a close-knit community with many friends. You may have trouble with power, natural gas, food, and other necessities from time to time, but you are protected here by your neighbors and community. I think you'll be fine, although I would prefer that you join me in Colorado."

Dr. Glenn looked at me with his stern, tranquil face. "Yeah, this is where I belong."

I smiled. He wasn't going anywhere.

"Peter," Dr. Glenn said, "tell me a little bit about yourself."

"He's an immortal. He was born before Jesus!" Julie spurted out to Dr. Glenn.

Peter and I both looked at her with astonishment.

"You didn't tell me it was a secret," she said with a mischievous grin.

"Well, it is," I said. "And don't tell another soul. I'm sorry, Dr. Glenn. Please let it stay in this room. Peter told me in confidence and now three of us know. Let's keep it our secret."

I looked at Peter with apology. "Sorry. This is as far as it goes."

"How old are you, Peter?" Dr. Glenn asked.

"Approximately three thousand years. I do not keep track anymore."

It was Dr. Glenn's turn to look astonished.

"He proved it to me on the drive from L.A.," Julie said with an animated expression. "He stopped breathing and his heart stopped! He might not be immortal, but he can die before your eyes, and then wake up!"

Dr. Glenn's eyes got big, and he raised his eyebrows in wonder. "Peter, can you die, or are you stuck here?"

"It is my choice," Peter said. "I can control the aging process. I will leave this body after the planet has transformed into the fourth dimension. But I want to stay for the birth of the next civilization."

"What's the fourth dimension?" Dr. Glenn asked.

"Hmm. It is hard to explain with words," Peter said. "The third dimension is what we are currently experiencing.

Chapter Four - Trip to San Francisco

The fourth dimension adds esoteric abilities, such as telepathy, clairvoyance, clairaudient communication with the etheric plane, energy healing, a feeling of oneness with God, and an overall spiritual feeling of tranquility. The fourth dimension will transform the planet into a completely new civilization."

"And how will this occur?" Dr. Glenn asked.

"It is already happening," Peter said. "Perhaps you've noticed time speeding up, where the day flies by? This will continue. Pay attention to it. The planet's energy vibration is increasing, as is ours. For instance, the human body is not solid. In fact, everything you see in this room is not solid. It only appears to be solid because it is vibrating at a high rate speed. The human body vibrates at around 80,000 cycles per second. Our bodies are just energy, as is everything. This is why people can disappear or walk through walls. If you think this is nonsense, then do some research on the yogis in India, who are perhaps the most advanced spiritual people on the planet.

"Our bodies will continue to increase in vibration in the coming years. Once we reach around 90,000 cycles, the truth will be released to humanity. Then, when we reach 120,000 cycles, war will cease, and peace on Earth will reign. Basically, the higher we vibrate, the more spiritually aware we become.

"This shift into the fourth dimension will continue and will become apparent over the next decade. Many will possess healing abilities, keen intuition, and other abilities not common today. People will begin to realize that something is happening to the planet, something profound. Not everyone will acquire fourth-dimensional attributes at the same rate. Today, as we speak, people are already tapping into the changing energy. Soon millions of people will be using these fourth-dimensional attributes.

"This is going to sound incredible," Peter said, "but our DNA is currently changing, along with the energy of the planet. With the changes to our DNA, we will be able to slow our aging and heal ourselves. Our DNA will become dynamic and intelligent. When people stop aging and stop getting ill, the proof will exist. Until then, all we can do is wait. One of the signs to look for is a proliferation of healing miracles, which is a sign of advanced spirituality. Also, when New Agers begin building healing centers and begin to have a major impact on society, fourth dimensional attributes will become the new normal.

"The plan for this planet is not evolvement, but transformation. We are literally going to change: our DNA, our beliefs, and our civilization. This planet is going through a rebirth, and we are here to experience it. Presently we are in the last days of the current civilization. Soon the rebirth process for the next civilization will begin. The birthing process will last less than a generation, but you can expect pain of that birth to be palpable for all to feel."

Peter stopped and waited for a reply.

Dr. Glenn seemed intrigued by Peter. He asked. "Is there anything we should do to prepare for this coming change? Should we form small groups and plan for the changes? Should we gather supplies that will be needed in the future?"

"Yes, I think so," Peter said. "Solar and windmill energy for backup power, along with battery storage. A water tank for backup. A greenhouse and a garden. A pantry filled with a month's supply of food. There is much that can be done. However, I think the most important thing to do is to prepare spiritually. Only those who are spiritually aware will come through unscathed.

Chapter Four - Trip to San Francisco

"Follow your heart and try to live as pure as you possibly can with a high degree of integrity. More than anything, just be. Don't think that you need to listen to others, instead listen to yourself, and have love in your heart. Be your own guide and realize that we are here to experience. We are not here to do anything. We are here to be, to experience this great miracle that we call life, to sit back and watch in wonder, to watch in amazement as the grand plan unfolds. Remember that God is in charge and that our lives are perfect, and everything will work out fine.

"Ideally, we each want to be a frequency of love. How do this? First, you need to keep your mind quiet. You do this by living in the present moment, observing your thoughts with an attitude of neutrality. No matter what happens in the present moment, accept it without a reaction. Stay neutral in a state of compassion, living with constant gratitude. Recognize that life only gives you two things: blesssings and opportunities. Everything else is a lie. All we get in this life are blessings and opportunities. That's the truth. Find the truth and you will be happy. Find the truth and it will set you free. Search for it. Few people search for the truth, when that is the holy grail. I'm 3,000 years old, trust me, I know what I'm talking about.

"When the world soon turns chaotic," Peter continued, "it will be too late to prepare spiritually. Instead, many will be frazzled and stressed. The better we prepare now, the more we will adapt and actually enjoy the experience of the transition. If you feel like joining a group that talks and plans for the future, that is fine. If not, that is fine, too. God will mobilize the lightworkers and create the transition as peacefully as possible. There are enough people listening to God's call. Follow your heart and be. That is my recommendation.

"Although, if you feel a strong desire to help with the transition, move to an area such as Colorado, Montana, or New Mexico and become involved in the New Age movement. This movement will have a huge impact on civilization. New Agers are creating the foundation for the next civilization. They are spreading the beliefs that will soon be adopted, and we can use all the help we can get. We will need doctors. That is why John has asked you to come to Colorado."

Dr. Glenn smiled at Peter. "If the near future turns out as you have predicted, I will consider joining you. But to be honest, I don't think the world is going to change as dramatically as you proclaim. We'll see."

"I'm coming to Colorado, too, if Dr. Glenn goes," Julie said. "Count me in after the economic collapse, and the widespread appearace of fourth-dimensional abilities."

I couldn't believe my ears. Here were two of my good friends, who I had not expected to see again in the future, and they were actually considering joining me in Colorado. How many more of my friends would join me, I wondered?

"Julie, if you come to Colorado," I said playfully, "will you go out with me?"

She smiled.

We had never dated, although we had spent time together as friends. She knew that I was attracted to her. I was afraid to spoil our friendship by asking her out on a date. However, I was hopeful that she might ask me out ... if I waited long enough.

* * * * *

Later that afternoon, Peter and I dropped Julie off at the airport for her trip back to Los Angeles. We had a group hug

Chapter Four - Trip to San Francisco

and said that we would stay in touch. She smiled, turned, and headed to the airline check-in counter. Peter and I felt grateful for the time that she had spent with us. It was really difficult to watch her go.

Chapter Five

San Francisco Lecture

The next day, Peter and I were scheduled to give our second lecture in San Francisco. In the morning, we met with a reporter from Seattle for an interview that our promoter had arranged. According to Stan, who was promoting the lecture tour, the interview would run in the *Seattle Post* before our visit the next week.

The interview lasted more than an hour. Finally, we had to end it, so that we wouldn't be late for our lecture. We kidded with the reporter that Seattle wasn't ready to read about metaphysical spirituality in their local newspaper. He smiled and said that the response would be interesting.

Peter and I arrived at the lecture on time. The large convention room was full, and a buzz of excitement moved through the audience. Music from Van Morrison played gently in the background. Peter and I made our way up the aisle to the podium. I approached the lectern and waited for Peter to turn off the music.

"Hello, everyone. Thank you for coming. I'm John Randall, your featured speaker. There will not be any detailed introductions today. We're just going to start. Sharing the podium with me today is Peter Vaughn. For the first hour, we will each give a lecture. For the second hour, you will be given the opportunity to ask questions. Peter will begin."

I left the lectern and sat in my chair ten feet away. As Peter passed me, I gave him a funny glance, and he smiled.

"Good afternoon," Peter said to the audience. "Today, I will speak about how we can create serenity in our lives. However, before I begin talking about serenity, I want to talk about beliefs. The beliefs that I am going to talk about are my own, and I do not expect you to agree with them. I feel that everyone has a right to their own beliefs."

Peter paused. "Do you believe that you are divine and that this lifetime is only one life in a series of incarnations? Do you believe that you are one with God and that no separation exists between you and God; in essence, that you *are* God? If you do hold these beliefs, then I can help you create serenity in your life. If you believe that you are separate from God, and that God will judge your fate, then I can't help you. Also, if you are an atheist, I can't help you, either. In both of those situations, fear will be the foundation of your life, and serenity will be elusive.

"Now that we have the prerequisites out of the way, I will begin. First, we have to understand free will. And guess what? Most of you have been misinformed. For, we do not have any, not in the sense that is generally understood."

Peter paused. "Most of you do not believe me. You think you have free will to make decisions and to live the life you want. I submit that you are naïve. For instance, tomorrow, try to do whatever you want and see what happens. The result, most likely, will not be serene. When I disregard my intuition, the result are problems that I have to deal with. I have learned from experience that I have to pay careful attention to my feelings, or else I create stress and anxiety.

"The question arises, why does our life go astray if we fail to heed the warnings of our heart? If we have free will, why can't we do what we want and still have serenity

Chapter Five - San Francisco Lecture

in our lives? The answer is, God is in control of our lives. We only think we are in control, but that is an illusion. We can either pay attention to God's will and have serenity, or we can do what we want using our free will, and create a mess out of our lives. Thus, free will is a misnomer. Free will is actually the ability to make a mess out of our lives. Free will is rebellion that always ends in tragedy, in one form or another.

"In many respects, I find myself enslaved to God, but that's not a bad thing. It's reality. This recognition proves that I do not have free will. Indeed, my life is controlled by God. I acknowledge that. And the more I become aware of God's control, the more aware I become that I do not have free will. That awareness leads to surrender, which leads to serenity. It's ironic, isn't it? Serenity comes from enslavement.

"When I learned that lightworkers did not come here to have fun, I was a bit angry. Everyone else is having fun. Why can't I? Well, it comes down to our soul blueprint. We came to help humanity, and that does not entail living a life of hedonism. So, our free will is curtailed in order for us to follow our blueprint. In fact, if we try to have fun using our free will, it will just backfire. Why? Because we signed up to help the planet transition, and our higher self is going to focus on that mission. Others signed up to have fun, but we didn't get those lucky tickets, those lucky blueprints. Sometimes, I wish I had an easier blueprint, but then I realize this is exactly what my soul needs at this time. In fact, life is perfect for everyone.

"Instead of free will," Peter continued, "we have choices. We perceive that our choices are free will, but that is an illusion. We have the free will to choose from a list of options that God defines, and not that these are defined in advance, before we are born into this lifetime. This is where serenity comes into play because we can choose to have serenity or anxiety. God allows us choice, but not free will. Free will implies freedom and individuality. But we are not free or independent entities. All of us are *one*.

"So, if God is in control of our lives, is it not advantageous for us to follow God's will? If you answer yes, then the next question is, what does God want from you? That is the question to ask yourself, if you want serenity in your life. Find out what God wants you to do. When your life is in conjunction with God's will, your life is serene. It's pretty much that simple. All you have to do is align with what God wants you to do, which is your soul's blueprint for this lifetime.

"The heart has a connection to God. The ego, which is limited to what it has learned in this lifetime, does not. In fact, here is a piece of ancient wisdom that has been lost: God communicates to us through our heart and ignores our mind. The heart is the gateway to the soul, and it holds our true intentions for this lifetime. What is important to understand, if you want serenity, is that these intentions originated before this incarnation. We are here to fulfill them. Does that make sense? I hope so.

"The mind and the ego are really superficial chatterboxes that just get in the way of our true intention. The ego thinks it has free will, but the heart knows that God is in charge. The heart knows that free choice is the opportunity to carry out God's will and fulfill our true intention, which is our life plan. We can choose God, or we can choose free will, which is rebellion.

"Now you know why the Bible says that pride comes before the fall. This is the pride that comes from arrogance, feeling puffy, and self-important. It manifests from the will

Chapter Five – San Francisco Lecture

of the ego. This type of free will will only get you into trouble and will never lead to serenity. Quite the opposite.

"The only free will we have occurs before we were born, before we incarnated. Indeed, we do have free will to make many decisions regarding each lifetime we choose. We get to decide what the soul needs to learn. After we are born, however, the constraints regarding free will dominate our lives. Remember when I said that we are all one with God? Well, before we are born, we actually plan as God. Does that make sense? Individuality appears real in our current lives, but when we leave our bodies and return home, it is a much different perception.

"Many of you may be confused. Let me just say that, before we incarnate, we are not as encumbered by our reality as we are on this planet. When we are not incarnate, we understand that we are God. We understand much more than we do when incarnate. It is as if the soul were blindfolded and made mute when we incarnate. Before we incarnate, we have the ability to make decisions on how our lives will unfold. We get to be part of the planning committee that decides which options will be allowed in our lives. Thus, each of us had a high degree of input into the formulations of our current lives.

"God is like a giant computer carrying out programs that were programmed by us before we were born. Today, in this very moment, there are reasons for our lives. We created those reasons in advance. Each of us has our own unique reasons, which we created and define *what* we came here to accomplish. Say to yourself, 'There is a reason for this life,' and know that it is true. The reason for your life is understood by your soul and by God. This reason is our life's purpose, and there are likely several reasons since life is so complex. Our life's purpose is not a singular thing. It can be complex with many intricacies, and integrate many incarnations."

Peter paused and scanned the room.

"If we want serenity, all we have to do is understand the reasons we incarnated. God's will is that we carry out the reasons we have chosen. This may sound difficult, but it really is not. What prevents us from understanding the reasons is simply not looking. People don't look because they are ignorant of the fact that God is in control of their lives. Thus, we do not perceive a need to find the reasons for our lives. Instead, we grope around, oblivious to God, denying that there are reasons. We live in our chattering minds, instead of in our hearts. We live for our egos, using our so-called free will and rebellion, while forgetting how indelibly involved God is in our lives. The mere idea of subverting our wills for God's will is noxious to the ego. The ego refuses to give up its glory, its identity.

"If you think that giving up cigarettes or sugar is difficult, try giving up your free will. It is not easy. Unless you are a mature soul or an old soul, giving up your free will is not even an option. Young souls are too enraptured with the ego to give up their free will. The thought of surrendering to God does not even cross their minds. They can't even perceive that they could be one with God.

"Young souls are adamant that they are separate from God. They firmly believe that they must lead their own lives. They believe the ego is real and is their means to salvation. They cannot perceive God controlling their lives. They perceive themselves in charge, and God as someone they will meet after this lifetime.

"It is interesting that young souls are usually the happiest people, although they are not serene. The reason for this is that they do not perceive God. Instead, they feel

Chapter Five - San Francisco Lecture

enraptured by their own sense of identity. They also do not feel the pain of the world. In essence, they do not have a conscience. The young-soul stage is spent learning lessons about the ego. During this stage, the focus of one's life is on self and identity.

"Remember the prerequisites I mentioned at the beginning of this lecture? Well, we must also comprehend that there is purpose, in other words, reasons for our lives. There is a reason for your life, and there is a reason for mine, and it is a specific one for this lifetime. And these reasons limit our freedom and our free will."

Peter stopped and took several gulps from his bottle of water.

"The only thing that prevents serenity is the lack of awareness of our life's purpose for this lifetime. What are you here for? Figure that out, and you can have serenity. Most people are not aware of God's impact in their lives. Thus, they are not aware that there is relevance to their lives, and a personal reason for this lifetime.

"Everyone on this planet has a different reason for being here. Each of us has different lessons that we are learning. That uniqueness is what creates our personal dharma. Getting in touch with that personal dharma is what serenity is all about.

"We need to be aware that God has a plan and that we have a role in that plan. When we understand our role, our lives can be serene. However, when we use free will to improvise, God's plan goes awry, as do our lives. As long as we can suppress our own will and surrender to God's will, we can have serenity."

Peter paused. "Some of you may think this is a simplistic view of life. It is, however, a fairly accurate representation, and I know from experience that it works. I have serenity in my life because I am aware that the reason I am here is to help humanity transition into a new civilization. That is my role. And I trust my heart, and not my mind, to show me how to help. I allow God to show me the way. I follow God's will and not mine. I do this, not only because I know that God can show me the way, but also because my way can never lead to serenity, but only anxiety.

"I am going to tell you how to create serenity in your life. Starting today, begin to notice each decision that you make. Then, using your intuition, notice if it is a decision that God wants you to make. If it is not, do not make it. Instead, begin to make decisions from the standpoint of God's will. Ask yourself what God wants you to do. In time, you will begin to understand your reason for this lifetime. You will also begin to make all of your decisions from the standpoint of your life's purpose.

"Try to do only those things that feel right and pure. Remember, the heart does not think; it feels. For instance, when you wake up, the natural thing is to take a shower and eat breakfast. In these situations, the thought process is on autopilot, with very little decision-making involved. Thus, you are not thinking, but feeling. Try to live your entire day this way.

"If your mind gets noisy, then observe your thoughts. Recognize that these thoughts are your ego trying to get your attention. Shut those thoughts off and stay in the present moment. You can shut them off by paying attention to your breath or feeling your hands. This connects you to your heart-center and shuts down the mind. The heart-center has priority of your attention, and the ego mind must wait for you to close the heart-center before it can have your attention. This is why people meditate. They open the heart-center and close the ego mind.

Chapter Five - San Francisco Lecture

"When something happens during the day that requires a decision, you have two places to find a response. First, you can use your ego and tap into your brain for a past experience. This is what we normally do. But, there is another option. We can open the heart-center and feel the possible consequences of your decision. We can ask our higher self the correct choice. We can ask how does your decision fit in with our life's purpose and with God's will? Is it in alignment? Is it rebellion? Is it ego? Or, is it something that is right and pure? Realize that your answer will lead to either serenity or anxiety.

"This may sound strange if you do not have a relationship with your higher self. But once you form one, you can ask your higher self anything. You will get a response via a feeling. Should I do this? Should I do that? Trust me, the higher self tell you!"

Peter nodded to the audience. "Thank you. I will be back for questions after John's lecture."

The audience applauded. Peter walked toward me, and I rose and met him with a handshake. "Are you sure you haven't been reading my books?"

Peter smiled. "Your turn."

I approached the lectern and looked out at the crowd. Peter had prepared them for what I was about to say. Now I knew why he was with me. It wasn't because I was bored with my lectures. He added a definite spark. He helped make the talks more enlightening and more exciting. During the first lecture, I hadn't known what to expect. But today, I was more relaxed and ready to use the opportunity that Peter had provided.

People generally did not know how to respond to my lectures. Now Peter and I gave a one-two punch, which allowed the audience the opportunity to become more comfortable with the message. One person can be easily dismissed; two are much easier to accept. Gazing at the crowd, I knew that I could say what I wanted to say without threatening anyone.

"Is everyone ready?" I scanned the room, letting the statement sink in, and then began. "The current civilization is no longer tenable. Over the next decade, the world will begin to transform. Today, I will talk about that transformation and what we can expect during the transition. Yes, transition. It will be a period of revolutionary and chaotic change.

"Many of you are interested in this transformation, also called the great shift. You have questions about what will happen in the near future. Well, I don't know the exact details of what's going to happen. I know only that our economic, social, political, and cultural systems will transform in a chaotic fashion. An imminent economic disruption will soon create a cascade of societal change. After the changes begin, the transition into a new civilization will dominate our lives for a generation.

"During this transition, we can expect our lives to change dramatically. Even that word isn't strong enough. Perhaps I should use the word radically. For, life as we know it will not exist for much longer. Get ready for major changes. Get ready for the world to literally transform into something completely different from our current way of life. It will be so traumatic that some people will feel like the world just turned upside down.

"Now, what will be the end result of this transformation?" I asked. "I bring you good news. No matter how bad it gets, the end result will be peace on earth. Yes, peace. That is what the transition is about: peace and love. During the early years of the transition, when fear and chaos are rampant, you may doubt this. I submit that there is

Chapter Five - San Francisco Lecture

nothing to worry about. Peace and love are the destiny and foundation for the next civilization. It has been ordained. It is God's plan.

"Currently, we live in the old paradigm, based on power and separation, which inevitably leads to conflict. In this old paradigm, we believe that we are separate from God and separate from each other. The new paradigm will be based on love and connectedness, which will lead to harmony. This is such a radical change that most people think it is a fantasy. And until the changes begin, only a small percentage of people are actually waiting for this new paradigm to take effect."

I paused and took a sip of water.

"The old paradigm no longer matters; it is irrelevant. Why? Because its days are numbered. The foundations of the old paradigm are on the precipice of crumbling. Why? Because they are based on lies, and the truth is going to begin to come out. Separation is a lie, and people are going to begin to realize this truth. The only thing that will remain standing is the truth. So, it is no longer necessary to fear those who seek to control our lives, such as government agencies or corporations. Those who covet power and control are powerless. They just don't know it yet.

"The new paradigm will look nothing like the old. The new power will be spiritual wisdom and truth. I know that sounds like fantasy, but in due time, we will all understand. The truth is that there is only one consciousness, which we all share. This truth changes everything. It dismantles all lies.

"So, what can you do now to prepare for this coming change?" I asked. "Spread the good news that there is only one consciousness and that peace and love are our destiny. Begin loving your eternal self and your fellow eternal men and women. Be grateful to God for the opportunity to experience the beginning of this beautiful new civilization. No matter how difficult it gets, be grateful. Recognize that life is comprised of two things: blessings and opportunities, and that everything else is an illusion.

"I have two specific things that you can do. First, find something to do that gives you joy, so that when you wake up in the morning, you have a smile on your face. Secondly, don't try to control the outcome of your life. These are perhaps the best two pieces of advice I can give you to prepare and live through the coming transition.

"Peter talked to you about serenity, and my advice about finding joy in your life is the same thing. To get through this period of change, we will need to have love in our hearts. It's people like you and me who will usher in peace and love. Our personal serenity is creating the mood for the next civilization. I can't emphasize this enough. Our serenity will create the next civilization. We will do it one person at a time.

"Nostradamus said that the foundation for the next civilization will come from the New Age movement in America. Well, I am a lightworker, and so are many of you. I know that he was talking about us. The New Age movement is about love, and we know about love. We know that love comes from within and leads to the awareness that everything is *one*. From this awareness comes compassion for people, for animals, and for the planet itself. We understand, better than most, that all life is part of God's consciousness.

"To a lightworker, the only thing that matters is love. Forget about work, politics, education, social status, and crime. Forget about it all. The only thing that matters to a lightworker is love. If you have love in your life, you have everything you need. Everything else is secondary. Everything else is of little importance.

Chapter Five - San Francisco Lecture

"The more you love yourself, the more it will be reflected back to you. The starting point for this is to love God with all your heart, with a sense of gratitude. And the higher you align, the more you will shine. So, love yourself and be an example. That is what a lightworker does. They spread light. They know that unity begins with self-love, and that the only way to create peace is to be the peace you want to see. Ideally, we want to be a conscious instrument of the divine presence. But this can only happen if we are in constant gratitude. This is not easy to achieve because gratitude is false unless it leads to virtue and integrity.

"The concept of love will be rewritten by the new civilization. How we love ourselves and how we love others will intensify in the coming years, as we become more aware of our divinity. We are the authors, and this is how it will be written: love and compassion are synonymous, and from love comes the concept of humanity. No longer will people have to prove their worthiness. People will be accepted and loved unconditionally based on the fact that we are *all* God. Nobody will be judged as lacking. Instead, everyone will be perceived as *perfect*.

"Civilization will be based on oneness. Thus, the foundation of civilization will be *love*. Today, we live in spiritual ignorance, and we perceive separation. Let's look at where that belief in separation has taken us.

"In Peru, in the 1990s, political terrorists were sentenced to enclosed, six-feet by six-feet isolation cells, with holes in the middle of the floors for toilets. They came out of isolation for thirty minutes each day. The people in power used this tactic to prevent the growth of revolutionary groups and to maintain their grip on power. This is only one example of how we have treated our fellow human beings under the old paradigm. The abuse of human rights has been rampant.

"During the Iraq war, from 2003 until 2008, Americans tortured Iraqis to extract information. If the so-called leader of the free world fell to this degree of depravation, how do you think other countries respected human rights?

"The last example I will give is the rampant racism that exists today. The current civilization does not perceive that we are indeed one big family. Instead, we treat strangers like enemies. Our level of trust for people of different ethnicity is pathetic. Recently, an Arab American Secret Service agent tried to fly during a heightened security period. When the pilot learned that an Arab with a gun was on the plane, he ordered the agent off the plane, refusing to accept his documentation as authentic. This type of prejudice is common today.

"Before this lecture becomes too political, let me return to the concept of serenity that Peter talked about. Serenity starts with the awareness that everything is divinely ordered. If you can perceive that everything is perfect, and that there are no accidents, you can be aware that all experiences are valid. The reason we have an experience is because God wants it so.

"If life is divinely ordered, then why complain to God that our lives are not always what we want? Why not just be grateful that God is giving us the opportunity to experience life? Some of you may be thinking that I am advocating passiveness, and I am. Life is changing toward passiveness. No longer will we be allowed to force our will upon others. In the near future, passiveness will be the key. There will be recognition that the world is divinely ordered.

"Those who attempt to use power to control others will find that it no longer works. Love is passive, and that is the way the world will be. When I say the world will be passive, I mean that people will be free to do what they want. People

Chapter Five - San Francisco Lecture

will passively allow them their free choice. People will live by the concept that everything is divinely ordered, and that maintaining peace and harmony has the highest value.

"Wars occur from aggressiveness, and war will steadily become non-existent as we move to a more passive approach. This probably sounds theoretical, so I will give some examples. In the near future, millions of people will leave California because of economic, social, and natural disasters. Many of them will gather together in less-populated states and create small communities out of nowhere, sharing their resources in order to survive. These will not be communist or socialist communities because politics will be diminished. Politics is about power and aggressiveness, and power will be replaced by love, which is passive. These communities will set an example of a new passiveness. Instead of an aggressive determination to rebuild society to its former self, these communities will take it easy and focus on harmony. And they will show others the way.

"Yes, leadership will be required. As in all social settings, a group of leaders will determine the rules and protocols of these small communities. Something new, something fascinating, will occur when these leaders are chosen because women will take on equal, if not dominant, leadership roles. One of the things the women will demand is equality, not just between men and women, but among everyone in the community.

"Do you begin to see the ramifications? Let's say there are a thousand people in one of the communities. Can you imagine the love that would exist among this group if they all treated each other equally? This is what I mean by passiveness. People in the new communities will not aggressively attempt to control power or social standing. Instead, they will passively accept their places.

"The women leaders will not allow aggression in the communities. They will not allow it because they know intuitively that aggression leads to power, and that the end result is disharmony and back to the way it is today. The women will create harmony by emphasizing a passive culture."

I took another sip of water.

"Aggression and a power-based civilization have provided enough trauma for this planet. If you tried to find one word to define the current civilization, power would be at the top of the list. God has decided it is time for us to evolve into a passive, love-based civilization. The overriding theme of the future will be harmony. We are going to use harmony as a basis for creating the new civilization.

"Passiveness comes from the awareness that everything is divinely ordered. Also, when we realize that we don't die, life takes on a new meaning. Why be aggressive when God is in charge? The people leading the communities will realize that it doesn't make sense to be aggressive. Conversely, harmony and passiveness will be the themes we live by.

"Love will also be a theme. This will lead people to be calm, relaxed, and even serene. Those who are aggressive will be a small minority. In such an environment, it will be easy for others to help them relax. Serenity will be much more pervasive than it is today and will have a much greater influence.

"We will not have to be aggressive and competitive to survive. In fact, we will use passiveness to survive. We will not gather weapons or aggressively defend our communities. No. In fact, over time, the new leaders will not allow weapons in the communities.

"Why passiveness? Why should we be passive when we need to rebuild civilization? The answer is God. God will

Chapter Five - San Francisco Lecture

show us the way. We will turn into an intuitive civilization. We will know intuitively how to live. Again, the key is harmony. For example, when someone in a community decides to open a business, he or she will first ask the community leaders if that business is needed. The leaders will then decide intuitively if it is needed.

"Today, if you want to open a business, all you need is money. It will be different in the future. Yes, you will still need money, but you also will need the community's blessing. Communities will be much more cohesive and interrelated. Resources will be spread wisely, with the intent to sustain the community.

"Another benefit in the future will be the lack of crime. Because communities will take care of their own, crime will not be necessary for survival. If you want to eat, you will have access to a meal. The same will apply for a place to sleep. With passiveness comes compassion and open arms. Communities will share what they have with each other.

"The new leaders are going to create communities that are personal, as opposed to the impersonal cities that exist today. People will feel as if they belong to their communities. A feeling of family will exist for all members of a community. Many small communities will have only one kitchen, and people will eat together in large tents or buildings. The community kitchens will provide a place where people can gather and talk. Love will begin to flourish as the lightworkers teach others that we are all one.

"Are you beginning to glimpse what I am talking about? The current belief systems that are the foundation of the current civilization are about to crumble. They will crumble because they have a false foundation. New beliefs shall emerge to replace the old, and old souls will show the way.

Many of these old souls will be children. As the Bible says, 'And the children shall lead them.'

"Yes, it will be the old soul children and young adults who understand that we are all one. These children will live by the new spiritual beliefs. They will be passive and intuitive, and they will create a civilization that is harmonious and joyful.

"I will finish my lecture with this thought for you to contemplate: When Jesus said, 'Not my will, but God's will,' he was talking about passiveness. We allow God's will by being passive. We follow our own will by being aggressive. Thus, are you an aggressive person or passive? Do you follow your will or God's will?"

I bowed. "Thank you. That's my lecture for today. Now we will answer any questions. There is a microphone in the front."

Peter remained seated. Several people began to form a line at the microphone in the aisle. A young woman in her twenties, squinting behind her glasses, asked, "This idea of passiveness and aggressiveness is confusing to me. Can you explain the difference?"

"Hmm," I said, "do you feel God intricately involved in your life?"

"No," she said.

"Well, that's your answer. Until you do, passiveness is not really an option. Until you feel God in your life, being passive won't work. But there is hope. You're here today because you have a spiritual desire to know God. I suspect you are going to hear God soon enough. Listen to your heart. You will know when God is speaking to you. It will come as a feeling." The young woman smiled and nodded and then turned to go sit down.

Chapter Five ~ San Francisco Lecture

"I will give one last example," I said to the audience, "of the aggressive nature of today's civilization, and the lack of humanity that goes with that aggressiveness. Watch what happens when the protests against the government begin. Watch how people, the non-protestors, react. They will request that any means necessary be used to halt the protests. People will call for the protesters to be arrested, if that is what is required to make them stop. This will be the aggressive last stand for our old way of life, but it won't work. Next question?"

A young teenage girl approached the microphone. "Is there a devil?" she asked.

I hesitated. "I'll let Peter handle this one."

He rose and took my place at the microphone. "I can only tell you what I believe. The answer is, no. I do not believe people go to a place called hell, presided over by a devil who has the power to control our will. And I do not believe there is a devil on this planet who attempts to steal our souls.

"If it were true that we can go to hell by being immoral or sinful, then hell would be a much more pervasive myth than it is today. And if hell did exist, it would be overflowing. Why would God send most of his creations to hell? After all, most of us are immoral when compared to Jesus, or a higher standard. Could there really be a moral cutoff point, where God determines that our soul has sinned too much? I think that is fantasy. It does not make sense to me and is contrary to everything I have learned.

"Personally, I think the concepts of a devil and hell were created to give the Catholic Church power. We are told that our only hope of escaping hell is to accept the Church. In essence, we are threatened with hell to make us accept God. The fundamentalists plead with us to come to Jesus, or else risk damnation. They tell us to avoid hell and instead choose eternal life. I think their ideas are relics of the past.

"Does God need to use fear and threats? Does that ring true to your ears? It never did to mine. Jesus' message, however, does ring true: 'Love.' Jesus said to love. In essence, he said that everyone is worthy of love. Indeed, he was preaching that God loves everyone equally.

"There is nothing in Jesus' message about fear or threats. If it were true that we are born at the mercy of hell, Jesus would have warned us. He would have preached about the devil incessantly. He would have told us that the devil has a right to our souls. However, this is not the case. All of that comes from the Old Testament.

"I believe the devil is a symbol of negative energy, such as hate, violence, and cruelty, which is the opposite of positive energy, such as love, compassion, and harmony. This planet has been enveloped in the duality of negative and positive energy for millennia. This duality has created a planet that lends itself to a myriad of experiences, both positive and negative.

"From God's perspective, everything is perfection. Thus, negative and positive energy are equivalent. Today, this is not accepted; indeed, it is blasphemy. This is what Jesus was hinting at with his messages. By consorting with the so-called sinners of his age, he was trying to show that God loves everyone.

"I tell you what I have learned: the only blasphemy is the denial of the divine. And since everything is divine, be careful what you deny as divine.

"Today, beliefs of the devil and God as beings have created the chaotic world in which we live. The fear of these two purported beings has preoccupied our minds. These beliefs have impacted society more than any other belief

Chapter Five - San Francisco Lecture

in history. From these beliefs, most people live in fear and judge their fellow men and women. Once we recognize that oneness exists, the preoccupation with separation will lose its hold. No longer will we view God as a being who is separate from us.

"The world's political and cultural systems are based on power and competition because of our belief in separation. No wonder the world today is chaotic, and conflict is an unending reality. It is sad that it has come to this. Currently, we live on the precipice of massive changes, all because of our aggressive nature. Even though these changes are imminent, people today are too naïve to notice that we live in an untenable situation. Maybe naïve is the wrong word. Maybe people are hypnotized or confused. I am not sure why, but I know that most people are naïve about the current situation that exists, and the transformation that is about to unfold.

"The irony of the current situation is amazing," Peter continued. "It certainly shows us that God has a sense of humor. Most people today live in a metaphorical bubble, completely oblivious to reality. The current civilization has agreed on a mass level, to forget who we are. We have agreed to believe that each person is separate. Such a belief has provided a bloody and anguished, although interesting, history. Not to mention, our strong belief in a devil.

"I do not mean to judge the current civilization. It has had its moments, especially the rise of technology. Many souls have had beneficial experiences. In fact, this planet Terra, as it is known on the etheric plane, is revered. Terra and the current civilization are a highly valued experience. If you have lived one life during this period, you are respected on the higher planes. The learning experiences that this civilization has provided are worthy of praise. However, the deep sleep that so many are in is about to change. The belief in a devil is about to end. Reincarnation will be accepted. The fear that is so rampant on this planet will also lose its hold. And, I might add, the religious institutions that have promulgated false beliefs are in their last days.

"I do not know how religious institutions will evolve, but I do not expect the religions of today to exist much longer. I agree with Nostradamus, who said that Christianity is in its sunset and would no longer exist in 2070. I also think the other world religions will evolve into a form that does not exist today. This will happen sooner than people expect."

Peter paused.

I rose and replaced Peter at the lectern. "That is all the time we have for today," I said to the audience. "Books can be purchased at the back of the room, and the MP3 of this lecture can be downloaded from my website. I recommend that you share them with friends. If you have any books to sign, I will be up front. Thanks for coming."

As Peter and I left the stage, I said to him, "That was very good. You have a knack for this."

He smiled. "Experience."

We laughed. Several people were waiting to greet us with more questions. We talked to the informal crowd for about twenty minutes and then made our exit.

Chapter Six

Trip to Seattle

The next morning, Peter and I packed my car with our bags and left for Seattle. We were looking forward to a successful conclusion of the tour. We had become close friends, and we both knew that Seattle would not be the last time we would spend together.

As we drove north on Interstate 5, I said, "I have another friend I want to visit on the way. She lives in Eugene, Oregon."

"Okay," Peter said. "Is she beautiful, too?"

"Attractive. Lucy is great. She lives with her son, Dillon. We'll stay at her house tonight. Tomorrow, we can spend the day with them."

Lucy was waiting for us at the front door. She smiled as we approached and met us with warm hugs. I introduced Peter, and she welcomed us into her house and asked about our trip. We found places to sit, and I told her how I had talked Peter into joining me on the tour.

Dillon was not quite two years old. He slept in his crib while we talked. Lucy said it was time for him to awaken, so it was okay if we talked. The conversation turned to children.

Lucy asked Peter, "If you're a wise teacher, what's the secret to being a good parent? What should parents teach their children?"

"First," Peter said, "let me compare the average American diet to being a parent. Currently, most people do not know how to eat healthily. The reason is because, for the most part, nobody knows better. People assume their food is healthy. Thus, they see no need to make changes. I can empathize. For the most part, no matter what they eat, they feel fine. They might gain some weight, but they still feel healthy. For the most part, people are healthy in spite of their diets.

"People eat multitudes of meat, dairy, sugar, and processed foods. They eat about a pound of meat every day and think nothing of it. Or they eat processed food, laden with chemicals and additives, every day, and think nothing of it. This is considered normal. Society questions people's diets only if they become obese. Otherwise, people think that any food is acceptable.

"The body is resilient and, for the most part, people remain healthy. So, people think it is okay to eat whatever they desire. Once in a while, a young, healthy person dies unexpectedly from cancer, but the general populace never attributes the death to diet. Yet, as I just stated, the average American consumes meat, dairy, refined sugar, and processed foods every day.

"So, the question is, should children be fed better? And should we, ourselves, eat better? The answer, of course, is yes. A good diet maintains optimum health, prevents potential cancers, and extends our life. Currently, society is beginning to change. Trader Joe's, Wild Oats, and Whole Foods, which all focus on organic food, are becoming popular. Holistic medicine is becoming more common every year. GNC nutrition centers are expanding, as people become more concerned with health.

Chapter Six - Trip to Seattle

"Slowly, people are beginning to perceive the importance of nutrition. Protein is still the most over-consumed nutrient, but hopefully, this will change soon. Protein should be restricted, not expanded. People should consume small quantities of meat and not large quantities. The body requires very little protein for optimal health. It is no coincidence that vegetarians are the healthiest people.

"Protein isn't the only thing vegetarians get right. They also eat a lot of fresh vegetables and fresh fruit, along with taking supplements. Only about 4% of the population are vegetarians. The rest of society could learn a lot by paying attention to what they consume. In the future, nearly half of the population will be vegetarian, and not out of necessity, but the choice of good health.

"Most vegetarians eat to live, whereas most non-vegetarians live to eat. There is a big difference. Most vegetarians focus on their health and consume what their body needs. Most non-vegetarians consume food for enjoyment. They don't realize that food is a temptation and that it is probably killing them. In many respects, people consume food like a drug, to satiate cravings. I would say food addictions are the most prevalent addictions in society today."

Peter stood and stretched. "Lucy, could I have a glass of water? That was a long drive, and I am a bit thirsty."

She rose. "Of course. I'm sorry, I should have offered you something. Can I get anything for you, John?"

"Sure," I said. "I'll take a glass of water, too."

Lucy returned with our water and sat down. "I'm glad you guys came. It's been too long since I've seen John."

Peter bowed his head and appeared to be praying to his water. After he finished, he drank several gulps.

"What did you just do, Peter?" Lucy asked.

"I purified the water using a blessing. Have you heard of the work by Masaru Emoto? He got this crazy idea of taking pictures of water using a dark-field microscope. The results are astounding. Go on the Internet and look at the pictures for yourself. If you bless your water, the crystals become beautiful. Without the blessing, the crystals look disjointed and disfigured. He even found that if you write the word 'love' on a bottle of water and leave it overnight, it will work just like a blessing."

Peter took another sip, then continued. "Okay, now that I have talked about the general ignorance of nutrition, let me make the statement that parenting, also, is woefully misunderstood. And, just like nutrition, it will evolve. As surely as we will begin eating better as a society, parenting will also improve. Thus, the question is, what is the problem with parenting today? I have outlined the problem with the general diet. Now, we need to ask, what is it that parents do not understand?"

Peter paused and looked at Lucy. "Do you understand the correlation?"

Lucy nodded. "I think you are implying that the obesity that is prevalent in society signifies the same problem with parenting. Not only are we eating poorly as a society, but we are also parenting poorly."

"Exactly," Peter replied. "First, parents do not understand the power of the child's soul and its interaction between the etheric and physical planes. In other words, a child is not alone. Their higher self is located on the etheric plane and is constantly monitoring them in a protective fashion. When you look at Dillon, do you see a helpless child, totally dependent on you? This is how the vast majority of parents perceive their children. But it is not so. Life is much more complex."

Chapter Six - Trip to Seattle

Peter paused.

"Wait," Lucy said, "I'm not quite sure I understand. I read John's books and other New Age authors, but it doesn't always sink in. Are you saying that Dillon's higher self can hear me from where it resides in heaven?"

Peter nodded. "Yes. The soul is split into many pieces, which are all connected and communicating. The core, or home base, of the soul, is on the etheric plane, or what call you call heaven. In fact, everyone's soul originates from the same source. From this source, the soul can break into pieces and expand its experience. It can literally live multiple lives simultaneously if it so chooses.

"One piece of the soul comprises our consciousness, which is sometimes called our aura. This consciousness is who we are and what gives us personality. This is why when people have near-death experiences and pop out of their body, they still feel like themselves. This is the soul that they brought into the body. And this soul has intelligence. Plus, it is closely linked to its higher self, which the body could not fully handle in its entirety. Thus, we are much more than meets the eye."

Peter smiled at Lucy to let her in on an important truth.

"Many people think that the entire soul is inside the body, but it is not. In fact, the soul is over the body, like a coat of energy. Although, as I just said, it is not the entire soul, but only a piece of it. This coat is a field of energy made of four pieces: the physical, emotional, mental, and spiritual. Think of it as the PEMS energy field as an acronym that is easy to remember. Each of these pieces has a function and a consciousness of its own. The soul on the etheric plane interacts with all four pieces. The truth is that you are interacting as much with Dillon's soul in heaven as you are with his memories since birth. Thus, there are many levels of intelligence."

"That's fascinating," Lucy replied.

"Currently," Peter continued, "this culture lives in spiritual ignorance. From this ignorance, we do not perceive the power of the soul or the interaction with the etheric plane. Once one begins to understand the power of the soul, the parenting style completely changes.

"Let me explain the power of the soul," Peter said. "The soul chooses its parents, personality, intelligence, life lessons, and so on, before birth. The soul has lived before, perhaps thousands of times, and understands what is about to occur in this lifetime. I cannot emphasize this enough. The soul is prepared. The soul is powerful. And most importantly, the soul is not based in the physical world.

"When I look at you, Lucy, I perceive a fragment of your soul. I see a part of you, not the whole. The whole is much more complex and powerful.

"When you look at Dillon, do you perceive that he is more than he appears? Well, he is more. Most of his soul is on the etheric plane and is in contact with him. It is the entire soul that makes decisions. The entire soul decides the lessons to be learned. People are much more than they appear to be.

"Dillon is not alone. Neither is anyone else. Not only do we have fragmented souls, but we have guardian angels who stay with us and give us guidance. Everyone has at least one guardian angel. Myself, I sometimes have twenty who travel with me. Alone? No, we are not alone."

"I sometimes wonder," Lucy interjected, "who is helping me. Sometimes, at the end of the day, I feel as if I had some unexplained help." She smiled. "There is something mystical going on that we are not aware of consciously."

Chapter Six - Trip to Seattle

Peter smiled back. "Yes, that is what I am talking about. We need to become consciously aware of this connection to the other side.

"Spirituality is about that connection," Peter continued. "Becoming aware of that connection is the key to parenthood. When I say that the culture is spiritually ignorant, I am saying that the vast majority of people are not aware of this connection. They do not understand that they are linked to their souls in heaven, which is then linked to God. People are not aware that each one of us is so complex.

"God has set up an intricate game of make-believe. No matter how vulnerable Dillon appears to be, it is an illusion. The game was set up so that a high degree of control was built in. So much control was built in that there are no accidents. In fact, everything that can happen already has. We are just playing back the possibilities. I like to use the phrase that everything is just rewind. God knows the future, or at least all of the possibilities.

"God is intricately involved in every instance of consciousness. So much so, that nothing can happen without God's approval. This may sound incredible and impossible. Yet, think of God metaphorically as a huge computer that controls everything. What connects everything to the computer is consciousness. In other words, anything with consciousness, and that includes *everything*, is connected to the computer. That is how God manages everything."

Lucy's eyes lit up. "We're all connected? Is that how it works? Life is one big matrix of consciousness? Wow, I never thought of it like that. If it's true, it's beautiful."

Peter smiled. "Yes, that is how it works. Let me give you an analogy. A baby is born. God knows about it. God knows the parents, the plans of the soul, and so on. Then, God monitors the events in the soul's life. If the soul decides the lessons are not going according to plan, the soul may make a request to leave the body through death. God contemplates all of the affected souls and makes a decision. If it is decided that other souls require lessons from this soul, then the soul is asked to remain incarnate.

"Most of the decisions are made on the etheric plane. In fact, nearly all decisions are made there. Do you see the implications, Lucy?"

She nodded slowly.

"We think that we have control of our lives," Peter said, "and that we are making our own decisions. However, that is not how life really works. Our entire soul, most of which is not on the physical plane, is actually making the decisions."

I added. "That's how the matrix of consciousness works. There is a constant interaction between all consciousness. We are all living *together*."

Lucy shook her head slowly. "Wow. This is intense. This is the direction of humanity, isn't it?"

Peter nodded. "Currently, Lucy, you perceive that you are the guiding force in Dillon's life. In fact, it is Dillon's entire soul that you are interacting with. And, I might add, his entire soul is very powerful. Once you are aware of the interaction taking place, you will begin to treat Dillon differently. For instance, you will begin to recognize that Dillon has his own plan and lessons to learn. Your job is to *allow* him to learn his lessons, and not get in the way. Do you see the difference from society's current perceptions?" Peter waited for Lucy's reply.

"Yes," she said. "Currently, parents perceive that it is our responsibility to teach our children how to live. We smother them with our beliefs. We tell them how to live. In effect, we do the opposite of what we should do."

Chapter Six - Trip to Seattle

Peter nodded. "Exactly. If current societal beliefs are so commendable, then why do we have so many social problems? Many teenagers are practically out of control. Thus, what we are teaching our children is not working. This recognition will lead to new modes of parenting."

"Well, what are these new modes of parenting?" Lucy asked.

"First, begin with the goal to empower Dillon, to give him an incredible level of self-confidence. Teach him Gnostic spirituality. Teach him that he is connected to God. Let him know that he is never alone and that nothing can happen in this life that he is not prepared for. Teach him that his beliefs and intent create his reality. And that if he wants a positive reality, then to remain positive. Teach him that his negative thoughts and beliefs pull him down. That they lower his vibration and fragment his energy field.

"Teach him the truth, that he is divine and that the divine only knows unlimitedness. The divine only knows wellness, success, joy, and aliveness.

"Teach him that if he believes something bad will happen, then it will. Teach him to only think positive thoughts and stay in that frame of mind. Teach him that joy attracts joy, and light attracts light. And to receive love, he must expect it. To attract a good outcome, he must expect one.

"Earlier, I said to teach him that his beliefs and intent create his reality. The reason why is because God is listening to our thoughts at all times. And God gives us what we ask for. This is what you need to teach him.

"After he is empowered through spirituality, teach him to be independent and how to subsist on his own. Teach him how to shop for food and how to cook. Teach him how to fix things and make things. Teach him how to clean. He should always be busy with projects. For instance, build a garden. Think of things to do besides sitting in front of the television or computer screen. Teach him photography, nutrition, how to preserve foods, and purify water.

"Of course, do not neglect his intellect. Make sure that he is good in math and English. Also, make him read constantly. Let him know that for life to be fulfilling, he must be a constant learner, and that reading is the foundation of learning new things.

"When the day arrives when he says that he wants to move out, hug him and say okay. If you do a good job of rearing him, he will not need your help to begin his life. This is the opposite approach of what is widely used today. Most parents do not empower their children. Likewise, children cling to their parents and lean on them for support and guidance. Parents often encourage this behavior and create insecure children who lack self-empowerment.

"A song by Sting has it right: If you love somebody, set them free. Children should be shown how to be set free and empowered. The role of parenting is not to teach children what *we* know. The role of parenting is to *guide* children to learn. We do this by teaching the children to think for themselves from the moment they are born.

"The worst thing that parents can do is to prevent their children from following their intuition. Never say 'no' unless you have an explanation that the child can understand. If you do not have an explanation, allow the child to learn from his or her *choice*. Parents should teach more by example and allow children to make their own choices.

"The relationship between parent and child should evolve quickly into an equal partnership. How quickly? Perhaps by one year of age. It is not long before children recognize that they are able to make their own decisions.

Chapter Six - Trip to Seattle

"Most people scoff at this type of parenting," Peter continued. "They say that young children cannot make decisions, or they will make wrong decisions. I submit that parents feel this way because they do not recognize the power of the soul and believe the child is powerless and naïve.

"Empowered children literally raise themselves. As parents, all we have to do is be their friends, and be there for them when they need us. We become their support group until they are ready to live on their own. We do not pester them with our own beliefs and expectations. We support them and allow them to make their own decisions. The only time we become involved in their decisions is if they ask for our advice.

"Once the Age of Aquarius is in full swing, parents will begin empowering their children. The results will be miraculous. Love will flourish as families empower their children, and the love will be felt deeply. Parents and children will recognize the divinity that they each possess. From this awareness, they will not judge each other. They will see themselves in each other, and they will recognize the *oneness* that exists. Do you see the implications?"

Lucy nodded. "It will be a completely new world."

Peter continued. "Once people become aware of their divinity, their parenting methods will change. They will begin to treat their children as equals and understand that it is their responsibility to empower their children. Slowly, as we evolve spiritually, we will begin to recognize the power and ability of children. Parenting will change significantly."

Lucy looked at Peter quizzically. "I understand what you are saying, and it's interesting. But how do I treat Dillon as an equal? He is just a child."

"By allowing him to make his own decisions. As a parent, you might be afraid to allow Dillon to make his own decisions, and you might not want to take the responsibility of him making poor decisions. In fact, you might believe that you are responsible for his decisions. Thus, your misplaced fear prevents you from allowing Dillon to make his own decisions."

"How do I let him make his own decisions?" Lucy asked. "He is two."

"Begin by giving Dillon choices for everything he does. Ask him what he wants for dinner and give him at least two choices. Teach him sign language, so he can respond. You will be amazed at his communication abilities.

"How do I teach him sign language?" Lucy asked.

"Use American Sign Language. This is yes." Peter made a fist with his right hand, then he moved the fist up and down with his wrist while his arm was stationary.

"No." Peter held up his open right hand with his palm facing Lucy. Then he closed the third and fourth fingers into a fist. Lastly, he brought the index finger and forefinger down to touch the thumb.

"Teach him a sign for now and for later. Then give him the choice to take a bath now or later. This is Now." Peter held out both hands palms up. Then he made a fist except for his thumbs and pinkies sticking out.

"Later." Peter made a fist, except for his forefinger and thumb, leaving a gun shape. Then he pointed the index finger at Lucy.

"After Dillon begins talking, continue to give him choices. Let him choose how he lives his life. Let him choose between going to the movies or staying home and watching a video. Always give him choices. This will give him power and self-esteem."

Chapter Six - Trip to Seattle

Lucy got up. "Let me get a pad. I want to write this down."

"He will learn quickly, believe me. He will show you the *no* and *later* signs faster than you can imagine."

We all laughed.

"Once you begin allowing Dillon to make his own decisions," Peter continued, "he will steadily assume more responsibility for his life. For instance, he will tell you when it is time to take a bath. Right now, you probably think I am nuts. But give it a try. See what happens when he begins making his own decisions.

"There will be occasions when you will have to give him advice," Peter added. "The key is to give advice, not to control. Do not buy a computer, and then force him to use it. Show him the possibilities and make it interesting. See if he is curious so that he can teach himself.

"If he does not want to learn to read, then read to yourself, thereby teaching by example. Then, advise him on the importance of reading. If Dillon still will not read, explain how reading benefited your life. Prove to him the importance of reading. Explain to him that reading is like breathing. That both are needed to live."

Lucy nodded. "Now I understand. It is my job to show Dillon the possibilities. Not to tell him what is good for him, but to allow him to choose on his own. If I guide him well, he will become a self-empowered gentleman."

Peter nodded and smiled.

"That was excellent, Peter," I said.

"Yeah," Lucy said, "I enjoyed it. I can't wait to begin teaching Dillon sign language!"

We laughed at her enthusiasm.

Chapter Seven

Seattle Lecture

Peter and I spent the next day with Lucy and Dillon and then left for Seattle the following morning. The drive from Eugene to Seattle was beautiful. The green rolling hills, trees, flowers, and blue sky enthralled us. The drive took the entire day, but we enjoyed it. We arrived in Seattle after dark and found our hotel.

The next day, at the lecture, the audience was large, with at least three hundred people. I had spoken several times in Seattle and had built up a large mailing list. Between the mailing list and the interview appearing in the local newspaper, I was not surprised by the large turnout.

Peter and I went on stage a few minutes late. In the background, Van Morrison played on a portable stereo. The crowd was noisy and in an energetic mood. I turned off the stereo and approached the lectern.

"Good afternoon. My name is John Randall. Peter Vaughn and I have been on a short lecture tour. Today is our last stop. We are both very excited to be here, and we appreciate that you came. Peter is going to speak first, and then I will follow him. We will answer questions after. Here is Peter."

I walked to my seat and grinned at Peter as he approached the lectern.

"Today, I am going to talk about *why* the world is about to change. This is important because when the changes begin, many of you will wonder what is happening. You will want to have some understanding. You will be searching for answers, looking for reasons. Today, I offer a few answers and reasons in advance."

Peter paused and poured water into a glass that was on a table next to the lectern. Then he took a sip and placed the glass back on the table. "All institutions will most likely fail. Economic, social, religious, political, and so on. Consequently, this civilization will likely collapse in its current form. As you can imagine, from this collapse, there will be anguish and emotional trauma."

Peter paused. "Before I continue, I want to state emphatically that if I was not 100 percent certain that we are living on the threshold of transition into a new civilization, I would not be up here today. Our destiny is to experience this new beginning, which will not be smooth. Instead, it will be a period of chaotic changes. These changes are the birth pains that we have to experience.

"When people around you begin falling apart emotionally, you will be able to help. You will be a pillar who knows why the transition is occurring. Whereas most people will be afraid of the changes, you will know that there is nothing to be afraid of. In fact, it will be a time to be joyous. For the outcome will be nothing less than peace on earth."

Peter paused and scanned the audience. They were in rapt attention. "First of all, it is not unusual for civilizations to collapse. That is how it works. It is quite natural for a civilization to fall. In fact, civilizations are meant to fall. It is the cycle of life. Today just happens to be one of those transition points.

Chapter Seven - Seattle Lecture

"Secondly, we are fortunate to be able to experience this transition. We should feel grateful for being here at this time. However bad it gets, we should feel grateful. This is an experience that we will cherish. We will tell others how we were on Terra when it transformed from third-dimensional reality to fourth-dimensional. Yes, four D. I will talk about that a little later.

"Okay, let us dig a little deeper. Why is the transition likely to be traumatic? The answer is because the last five thousand years have been violent and destructive. The destructiveness has been recorded and is lurking in the mass consciousness. How many wars have there been in the last five thousand years? Too many to count. How many wars are currently being fought?

"Nothing happens that is not recorded by the Creator, or God, if you prefer that term. And not only is an event recorded, but it is remembered and has ramifications. This is why we will have a turbulent transition. We have created a mess, and now we get the outcome. Thus, the exit point is not going to be smooth."

Peter paused and took a drink of water.

"God is *all*. Thus, there is only one consciousness, which we all share. This is a difficult concept to grasp on this dense planet. Essentially, because of the interconnectedness of consciousness, all events affect other events. There is a Chinese saying: 'A breath can affect the flight of a butterfly on the other side of the world.' In other words, a thought can affect the future, and so can an action.

"The current civilization has built up an inordinate amount of karma. These are the ramifications of the last five thousand years that are impacting the transition. This is why so many people have predicted trauma for the end of this civilization. The great memory bank is called the Akashic records. People who are able to tap into this record book can theorize that something severe is going to happen.

"The future is full of possibilities, but the past eventually comes to bear on the future. One who is able to know these possibilities can guess what is going to happen. Many people have guessed that something traumatic will happen soon. The timelines are all coming together, and it is becoming easier to guess the future.

"The current civilization will soon fall and will be replaced by a new one, which will be the fifth, and last, on this planet. The new civilization will last approximately six thousand years; then it, too, will fall. After that time, this planet will no longer be inhabited by incarnate humans or other aliens. Terra will be left alone, to carry out her remaining years in tranquility. The animals get to stay, but we have to leave. Why? That's God's plan. Terra is going to become a paradise for plants and animals. The Garden of Eden. A nature preserve."

Peter paused and then pointed to his chest. "What is a body? Is it us? In the grand scheme of things, a body is nothing more than a temporary vessel which is used to incarnate for a short period of time and then discarded. The body is nothing more than a collection of cells inhabited by a soul. You may feel uneasy with such a metaphor, and I understand your concern. However, my motive is to impress upon you that we are God. We are the part of God that is inhabiting the body, which is our soul.

"My point is that we do not need this planet in order to exist. We can incarnate on other planets, in other civilizations. Life is about much more than one single planet or one civilization. Therefore ... so what if this civilization is transforming? It is not something to get all panicky about. Remember, everything is already perfect as it is. If it

Chapter Seven - Seattle Lecture

were not, then it could not be God. We are here, so let us experience it. Let us experience it from the context that we are divine souls, and that life is divinely ordered.

"Another point I want to make is that even though the next civilization will be more enlightened, that does not make it better. Yes, we experienced negativity to a high degree during this civilization, but that does not mean that it was worse. Some lessons can only be learned in a civilization that provides negative experiences."

Peter took another sip of water.

"What is the result of a lifetime spent experiencing the negative? One lifetime is of little consequence in the grand scheme of things. Charles Manson, John Wayne Gacy, and Adolf Hitler lived lifetimes that did not destroy their souls. Why? Because one lifetime cannot destroy the soul. Several negative lifetimes in succession can result in regression, but that is rare, and the soul is given many opportunities and support to evolve.

"The souls we judge to be damned for their behavior are no different from us. External judgment does not exist with regard to our souls. Judgment exists only for us personally. We judge ourselves. There is no God that judges us, because *we* are God. The only God that exists is the totality of everything, the singular consciousness. God is not a being, unless you want to consider the totality a being, which makes no sense.

"The current civilization is confused and naïve with regards to spirituality. But then, it has to be, if people like Hitler and Charlie Manson are going to be historical facts. We actually created this confused civilization on purpose. We wanted to experience extreme duality, and it has worked splendidly. The array of experiences that we have created is incredible. People have had the opportunity to do things in complete blissful ignorance.

"I repeat, this has been a splendid civilization. Everything about it is perfect. Not one life has been imperfect or wasted. We created duality, and it has worked to perfection. As perfect as it has been, however, the vast majority of people now live in utter confusion regarding spiritual truth. This confusion is finally coming to an end. It probably would have continued onward if it wasn't for the fact that we were on the verge of destroying civilization with our negativity. We reached a point where we either had to change or else civilization was doomed.

"The next civilization will not be confused, because spiritual truth will be known. It will be a fact of life. In fact, it will be a way of life. Everything, from social norms, economics, politics, and healthcare will be based on spiritual truth. People will know that we are God and that we are eternal. Today, there is ambivalence about the concept of eternal life. And there is outright hostility toward our divinity. However, this will change in the near future.

"The reason it will change is because of fourth-dimensional consciousness. Soon, the energy on the planet will allow many to communicate telepathically, heal themselves using their minds, and age very slowly. This new energy will also allow us to feel a connection with one another. Most of us will become consciously in contact with our higher selves. Energetic healing will become the norm, because people will be able to see into one's aura to identify energetic imbalances.

"This fourth-dimensional consciousness will usher in a new spirituality. New spiritual truths will spread, and we will spread the word. You are here to spread these truths because you are a lightworker. You are a teacher of truth.

Chapter Seven - Seattle Lecture

Lightworkers have been spreading this message for decades, and we have been outcasts and pariahs for our efforts. However, our love, vision, and knowledge will prevail. As the saying goes, truth will always prevail.

"The transition is about rebirth. Yes, there will be chaos and trauma, but that is not something to fear, just something to experience. In fact, it can be a joyful experience. All we have to do is be aware of the beauty of God's grand scheme, and recognize that these are just birth pains.

"Let us delve into the mind of God. God is constantly processing all of the input of everything, and this input creates ramifications. Since God is perfect harmony and love, that is the basis for moving forward. So, the result is that the output is guided toward harmony and love. This is why we are transitioning. We now need to move toward harmony and love.

"It may not appear this way, but that is indeed the truth. God does allow civilizations to create disharmony for too long. Note the last five thousand years, which saw the demise of the Mayan, Egyptian, and Roman Empires. God allows us to create civilizations and learn from our experiences. However, because God is harmony and balance, God can tolerate only so much imbalance before harmony is restored. Note that if this harmony cannot be restored, some type of ending will occur.

"From this natural inclination towards harmony, comes the myth that God's wrath manifests when we create too much disharmony. To a certain extent, this myth is true. The truth is that civilizations rebalance themselves. Civilizations have a mass consciousness, and this mass consciousness is always trying to create harmony and love. Our civilization is extremely out of balance, and now a major adjustment is required.

"I know that this is heady stuff, and you may be shaking your head in confusion. Please know that we created this civilization as a group. Most people think that they do not have an impact on society, but this is not the case. Everyone has an impact.

"Our thoughts impact other's lives. We create together. There is real power in beliefs and thoughts. Anything happening on this planet is happening because people are creating it. This is little understood. The fact is, our beliefs form consensus beliefs, which have profound effects. Thus, civilizations are true democracies. They are democracies of beliefs."

Peter paused and scanned the audience in deep thought.

"When the changes begin, most of us will accept these changes without much resistance. We will realize that what is happening is needed and that a better way of life must be created. From these beliefs, harmony and love will be restored.

"What we are going to experience is the birth of a new civilization. We are very fortunate to be here to experience this incredible event. In fact, we all have a front-row seat, for which we should be grateful. If we understood the magnitude of what is about to transpire, we would cry like little babies at our fortune to be alive at this time."

Peter nodded. "Thank you. I will be back for questions in a little while. And now, here is John Randall."

The audience applauded, and Peter went to his chair. I rose and went to the lectern, grinning at Peter as I passed.

"I'm going to change the subject," I said to the audience, "and talk about philosophy. Peter gave you answers, and that's my aim as well. When the changes begin, you likely will search for answers to questions that you presently don't even ask. For instance, how often do you question why you

Chapter Seven - Seattle Lecture

made a particular decision? When life is relatively easy, we make decisions without thinking twice.

"In many respects, decision-making today is from conditioned responses: we do what everyone else is doing. This kind of decision-making works today because there are rarely ramifications for following the status quo. When we need a television, we just go to a store and buy one. We don't think twice about it because that's what everyone else does. We go home, plug the cord into the wall, and press the remote. We sit down in front of the TV, and we don't think twice about the purchase. It's over.

"This kind of decision-making is dominant in the current civilization. We all agree to live in certain ways. We agree to play certain roles. There's nothing wrong with this kind of behavior, but it's about to come to an end. Once this civilization begins to fall, the decision-making process will change. No longer will a simple decision, such as buying a television, not have any consequences. No longer will we be safe to follow the masses, although many will try. What used to work for our decision-making is no longer going to work. The status quo is going to break down.

"In fact, a new philosophy will be required for us to survive. The new philosophy is what I want to share with you today.

"Let's start with a statement made by Krishnamurti: 'It is only the mind that is confused that chooses; but for a mind that sees clearly, there is no choice.'[3] He was implying that we never have to make a decision with our mind. Instead, we can use our feelings, our heart-center, which is connected to our higher self.

"What, you might ask, does this mean? It means that our choices should be intuitive. For instance, when you wake up in the morning, do you think about taking a shower, or do you feel like taking a shower? This is the philosophy of the next civilization. Currently, a small minority of people live this way. In the future, everyone will live like this.

"Why will we change? Why will we make decisions with our feelings instead of with our minds? Because the mind uses images based on the past and the future. This will no longer lead to good outcomes. Instead, we will need to live in the present moment, connected to our soul and our higher self.

"You might ask, if this is the best way to live, how come so few people use this kind of decision-making? Because, today it is advantageous to use our mind, and to be logical if we want to be materially and socially successful. The current civilization is based on competition, and the competitive environment requires that we use our mind to make decisions. Today, we have to play the game. If we refuse to compete, society allows us to achieve only so much. For those of us who opt to play our own game, we are left to fend for ourselves. That usually means a simple lifestyle as a pariah, or an outsider who is tolerated.

"Most people want to fit in and, thus, agree to compete. This is where the mind dominates decision-making. Most of us make decisions from the standpoint of maintaining or advancing a certain standard of living. Now, I'm not begrudging this kind of decision-making, which is the Tony Robbins, Ayn Rand philosophy of individualness. I'm simply stating that it works in the current culture.

"People who use their minds can achieve. It's as simple as that, in today's environment. For this reason, the majority of people rely on their minds for decision-making. People use images in their mind to determine their decisions. If an image conjures up potential loss, the decision is rejected.

Chapter Seven - Seattle Lecture

If an image portends maintenance of the status quo or advancement, then it is accepted.

"Let me give you an example. A friend who is wealthy and has connections that can advance your business, invites you and your spouse to a party. You know that if you go, opportunities might arise; thus, you want to accept. Your spouse, on the other hand, has made other plans for the evening, which you have already accepted. But it's a party with your friends, and you've been there, done that. The other party has huge potential for your career, and you want to attend.

"An argument with your spouse erupts as you attempt to change his or her mind. Your spouse wants you to make money and provide a comfortable lifestyle, but doesn't want you to bring your work into the relationship. Your spouse is adamant that you have already made plans with your friends. However, your mind, which is your ego, wants to make your business more successful. Your mind, and its images of the future, drive you to argue with your spouse.

"The argument isn't about money. It's about images. Your spouse has an image of smiling and enjoying the party with her friends. You have an image of schmoozing with contacts and feeling important, expanding your business, and becoming more successful. Once you begin making decisions with your mind, images dominate.

"The winner of the argument is the one who can control the spin of the images. You try to convince your spouse that this is an opportunity for both of you. You create images of prosperity and happiness. If that doesn't work, you try to convince your spouse that this is important to you, and that they should do it for you, or else there will be ramifications. This creates a guilt trip, along with images of the relationship floundering.

"Your spouse, on the other hand, smothers you with images of his or her unhappiness, threatens to withhold love because you're not loving correctly, and impresses on you the images of a relationship in tatters."

The audience laughed. I paused and poured myself a glass of water.

"You can see the mess that can happen when images are used for decision-making. Conflict is always lurking. Anytime people in a relationship have conflicting images, conflict can arise. I'm not just talking about sexual or marital relationships. Any relationship, be they friendships, work-related, or school-related, can have these conflicts.

"Anytime you have to make a choice, there can be conflict. This example illustrates a conflict with two choices that most people would agree are valid choices. But conflict can exist with any choice that the mind must make. This is why Krishnamurti called this the mind in confusion. We have to get out of the mind and into the heart, which knows the right path.

"Conflict is a creation of the mind. As I said, today we use our minds to live. In the future, we will use our feelings. We will give up conflict and, instead, love one another. Rather than argue, we will smile and love each other. We will allow people to do what they want, without images of how their behavior will affect us.

"So, how could this example be handled peacefully without conflict?

"In this example, you and your spouse could have gone to separate parties. Initially, you might have suggested that you both accept the second invitation. Then your spouse would have suggested that you attend the second party alone, if that was what you wanted; your spouse would attend the first party, as already planned. You would have

Chapter Seven - Seattle Lecture

agreed. You would tell each other to have fun, and you would trust each other to attend the separate parties.

"You see the difference? You both follow your feelings, and you allow others to follow theirs. You keep the future images out of your mind and stay present, out of the ego. You do not choose one of the two parties, so there is no conflict. Conflict arises when we believe that we have to choose, which creates a consequence.

"As you can imagine, this type of change in society will entail a revolution in our way of thinking and living. This is how we're going to change as a civilization. We'll begin thinking differently and acting differently by using our intuition instead of our ego."

I paused and took a sip of water. "Contemplate what is coming. Ask yourself seriously, how will you adapt to this change? How will you change the way you currently live?

"Some of you may be confused about what I'm saying, so I'll give another example. Let's say that your teenage son is a musician. He doesn't care about school, and his grades are terrible. On a positive note, he does not drink or use drugs. As far as you can determine, all he wants to do after high school is play in his band and live at home. So, what will you do?

"Your spouse is an artist who reveres independence and artistic creation and supports your son's pursuit of music. On the other hand, you abhor your son's lifestyle. You want him to go to college and get a degree, to find a real job that will support him. In your opinion, music will never lead to anything meaningful.

"In this atmosphere, a conflict erupts, a conflict of images. You have an image of a son who sits around and plays music and accomplishes nothing. You refuse to allow him to make his own decisions, and you don't accept the decisions he has already made. The conflict comes from the future image in your mind, and that image is unacceptable.

"What's the result? The conflict creates a chasm between you and your son, possibly even creating a permanent separation. Rather than a relationship based on unconditional love, you have conflict.

"Do you see where the logical mind and its images get you? You're on the precipice of losing your relationship with your son. All because your image of him isn't worthy from your standpoint. Are you ready to lose your son just because you don't think he's worthy of your unconditional love?

"These are the kinds of conflicts that occur when we use the mind for decision-making. In the future, people will come to this realization and will stop using logic, ego, and societal norms. This won't happen all at once. It will be part of the shift, part of the transformation."

I paused and took another drink of water.

"As society collapses and begins to transform, people will begin adapting to the changes. Many will begin living in small groups for sustenance. These small groups will be egalitarian, with many women assuming leadership roles. In these groups, people will discuss how to reorganize society and how to live.

"The issue of harmony and conflict will be foremost in their minds. They will want to avoid the conflicts that are currently so pervasive between people and groups. They will want everyone to get along peacefully with each other so that there is harmony in their community. They'll know that love is the key, and that unconditional love must play a vital role in their community. I do not know how this is going to unfold, but I do know that love will be the foundation of society, and the next civilization. It is going to replace power and become the new central theme that we all abide by.

Chapter Seven - Seattle Lecture

"When we love unconditionally, there is no conflict. This will be apparent in the future when people begin looking for answers to our problems. Currently, we're not looking for answers on how to live in harmony. Instead, we're looking for ways to make more money, or to maintain what we have. We're stuck living a way of life that creates conflict and very little harmony. This is about to change."

I paused and took another drink of water from my glass.

"Because I'm talking about images, I want to discuss fear and love. Let's begin with fear. Fear is a negative thought or image created by the mind of a potential future event.

"Do you know what the letters stand for? Fear, F-E-A-R, is False Evidence Appearing Real.

"Fear is always about a possible future event that has not yet occurred. Thus, fear is an idea. In fact, fear and the truth cannot coexist. Why? Because everything is perfection, and the divine can only know perfection.

"Fear is the result of the mind refusing to live in the present moment. When we live in the present moment, fear is impossible. We might experience pain in the present moment, but not fear.

"Contrary to popular belief, fear is not an emotion. Emotions can only be experienced in the present moment. When we fear a potential future event, we *create* emotions such as anguish or anxiety. Do you see the difference? We create fears, which lead to emotions. Ironically, there's nothing to fear, and only events to experience. Events are valid and perfect and occur in a divinely ordered universe. In fact, the only two events that we ever experience are blessings and opportunities. Everything else is an illusion.

"Now, let's look at love. Love, unconditional love, isn't an emotion either. Love is who we are. It is our beingness, our core. This will take some explaining, but I'll try to clarify.

"Unconditional love is not really understood at this time. That's to be expected, however, considering how spiritually immature we are right now. Most relationships are based on images and not on unconditional love. Images and roles are basically the same thing. When we subconsciously agree to play a certain role in a relationship, the other person places an image of that role in their mind. The images that each partner holds determine the dynamics of the relationship.

"These images, which are used in place of unconditional love, create emotions through the release of chemicals in the body. We are literally addicted to each other by our images, which make us feel 'in love.' If the images change, then the chemicals no longer make us feel 'in love.' This is what we call love today.

"This type of relationship is actually restrictive and is filled with conflict. Thus, relationships that exist today are inevitably filled with conflict, unless it is a relationship of a rare couple who have found unconditional love. Some of you are nodding in agreement. The rest of you probably wonder if I'm right. Could nearly all relationships that exist today be filled with conflict? This doesn't seem possible, but it's true. Why? Because of decision-making with the mind, where images and conflict go hand in hand.

"Because unconditional love is our core, we naturally love everyone, unless we conjure images to negate that love. It is only cultural conditioning that removes our intuitive love for other human beings. We deny this love today, but that does not make it any less real. The reality is that we are all one, and, with this awareness, we come to realize that we love ourselves, as well as everyone else. In fact, the starting point is learning to love ourselves, then we can love others. We like to think that we choose whom we love. In fact, we

Chapter Seven - Seattle Lecture

choose whom we share our emotions with, and not who we love.

"Unconditional love rarely exists today. Unconditional love means just that, no conditions. It means allowing another being to make his or her own choices without our judgment. However, because our current civilization lacks spiritual awareness, nearly all relationships lack unconditional love. Instead, relationships are based on images – which replace unconditional love – of what is allowable or acceptable. Today, we place conditions on each other, and we live by conditional love.

"Earlier, we examined the spouses attending a party and the wayward teenage son. The two examples I gave demonstrated the lack of unconditional love in society today. They also demonstrated the conflict that exists when unconditional love is absent.

"In conclusion, to have a relationship based on unconditional love, we can't have images of what we expect from each other. You may be thinking that this is impossible today, and you're probably right. But, in the near future, it will be possible. In fact, unconditional love will flourish."

I pointed to the microphone in the middle aisle twenty feet away. "Okay, it's time for questions."

People began walking forward to the microphone. The first person to arrive was a woman about forty, with long, curly brown hair and brown eyes.

She looked at Peter. "You said that not one life is wasted or imperfect. This implies that we're perfect manifestations of God. That sounds good in theory, but when will I feel like a perfect manifestation? Today, I feel very alone, with plenty of guilt and fear."

I stepped aside, as Peter approached the lectern.

"Sooner than you think," Peter said. "During the transition, people will begin accepting new beliefs as fourth-dimensional energy begins manifesting. It will soon become widely understood that we are all manifestations of God and that we are all divine. I agree with you that this concept is currently only an ideal for most, but have faith. In the near future, it will be the norm. Once a critical mass becomes aware that we are divine, nearly everyone will begin treating each other accordingly. Once that happens, you will feel like a perfect manifestation."

Peter paused and then said, "Next question?"

A bald, middle-aged gentleman approached the microphone. "I have a question regarding earth changes. When will they intensify? And are Mount Rainier and Yellowstone going to erupt?"

Peter looked at me, and I pointed back to him to answer.

"We are right on the precipice of earth changes intensifying. Look for floods, drought, tornadoes, strong winds, earthquakes, hurricanes, and volcanoes.

"Yes, Mount Rainier will erupt soon. Thankfully, Yellowstone will not. I am sorry to inform you that Seattle is threatened. The Native Americans have a prophecy about Mount Rainier: 'When little sister erupts, big sister will follow.' Little sister was Mount St. Helens.

"Also, Seattle borders the ocean. I do not suggest living in any state that borders an ocean anytime after 2026. Coastal areas will be subject to severe flooding. Sometime between 2027 and 2037, oceans will be inundating many areas in the United States. If you feel unsafe where you live, I recommend moving. Next question?"

A young lady in her early twenties approached the microphone. "You said that we created civilization. Who is we?"

Chapter Seven - Seattle Lecture

Peter paused and contemplated. "Hmm. This is a big topic, but I can give you the short answer. When I said we, I meant souls just like you and me. We created all of the third-density life forms that exist. The entire physical plane is created by us, the plants, animals, elements, everything, even planets and stars.

"Currently, people believe that God created all of these things. However, God's creations include us, and we have creative abilities, too. God allowed us to create the physical plane. Understand, we are God. Nothing we do is done in a vacuum. In other words, we do not create without God's input, and God is intricately involved. To understand this better, you might read John's books.

"Anyway, we create planets and life forms. Then, we intricately create civilizations and populate the planets. Do you not think this is possible? Our civilization is not very technologically advanced, yet we are already able to clone animals. Do you not think we could genetically engineer a life form after a few millennia? Think about cloning. All scientists start with is a cell, and boom, there is a life form. It is not that complicated once one understands the process.

"Planets are not as easy to create, but we do know how. Right now, as I speak, souls are contemplating the creation of new planets and new civilizations. This contemplation is occurring on the etheric planes of existence, not on the physical plane. Those souls are not incarnate as we are at this moment. "Currently, with our incarnate bodies inhibiting us, we have no idea of our wisdom and abilities. Souls, like you and I, have incredible abilities. Yes, we can create planets. And, yes, we do create civilizations."

Peter continued and leaned forward intently. You could feel the passion in his voice. "We are the courageous souls who decided to incarnate and experience our own creations.

To be alive at this time is a very courageous act. We do not realize just how courageous we are. We will all have enormous joy after this experience is over and we leave the planet. We will celebrate this life. One of the things humans like to do is have parties and celebrate. Where do you think that came from? One of the things we do on the other side is a lot of celebrating. And celebrating an incarnation is a common thing. It's like celebrating all of our birthdays all at once.

"Death is not about a life ending. It is about moving on to new experiences. Leaving this planet is about starting a new phase, a new adventure. It is not something to be afraid of, but welcomed. That said, I want to be emphatic that suicide is not an option for leaving this planet. That is not something that will be celebrated. It is the one thing that God does not look kindly towards. The most serious karma, by far, is obtained through suicide. I repeat, it is not an option. Or, to be more precise, it is the worst option for leaving this planet. Why? Because it upsets the agreements that have been made and the path or journey of the soul. It is debilitating not only to the soul who chooses this escape, but other souls who are dependent on that soul."

Peter paused. "I seemed to have digressed from the original question, which was about creation. But when I said death should be welcomed, I did not want to give the wrong impression."

Peter took a drink of water. "Let me finish my original answer. I only had a few more thoughts. We create multitudes of planets and civilizations, because we want to have a wide array of experiences. And because we are essentially love, most of the planets and civilizations are harmonious. There are some planets that are not harmonious and avail themselves of negative experiences. Earth is such

Chapter Seven - Seattle Lecture

a planet. Here on Earth, we can experience a vast array of negative experiences. Believe it or not, this is good for our soul. It allows us to see both sides of the fence, the positive and the negative.

"Those of you who are squirming with unease at this concept of no morality have experienced the very things that you refuse to embrace. It would not surprise me if everyone in this room has killed an adversary in one lifetime or another. In fact, that is what I would expect. As the saying goes, we all have dirty laundry.

"To conclude, we create inharmonious planets on purpose. The events that have unfolded on this planet, and the events to come, were planned for a purpose. It is all perfection, and all part of the grand plan. The intricate web that exists in life is beyond our wildest imaginations."

Peter turned toward me. "I think I had better let John answer some questions now."

I rose and went to the lectern. "He's a tough act to follow," I said to the audience. "Next question?"

The next person in line was a teenage boy with shoulder-length blonde hair and a few pimples across his face. "It sounds like the future will be boring," he said, "if everyone loves each other."

"To a certain extent, that's true," I said. "Life will be boring because there won't be a lot of surprises. We won't hear lurid stories about crimes and celebrity scandals. The variations of experience will be curtailed once negativity is limited. There won't be much entertainment, sports, or gambling. There won't be very many exciting things to do.

"On the other hand, we'll have the opportunity to love one another and live in peace and harmony, and we won't live in fear. Love will be pervasive, and we'll enjoy the feeling. To a large extent, we'll simply be happy. We won't need excitement.

"One area that will not be boring is human relationships. As a civilization, we're currently in the mature cycle, which is focused on emotions and relationships, and this cycle will last for quite a long time. Sexual relationships will be particularly interesting. Soon, we will no longer consider sex a taboo. In fact, sex will be considered as natural as eating, and very useful in maintaining good health, since it rebalances our individual energy fields.

"Likewise, people won't restrict themselves sexually, as they do today. People will be open and communicative with regard to sex in the near future. There will be a burst of sexual freedom, not unlike the 1960s. And because love will be the foundation of civilization, it will be much healthier and emotionally satisfying sex. In fact, sex education will be all the rage, as people desire to learn how to have safe sex.

"People will be able to use drugs if they desire, but few will after the transition. The people who survive the transition will be advanced souls and will know intuitively that harming the body isn't a wise thing to do. A healthy orientation will be the norm. When someone does use drugs or alcohol, it will be accepted by the people around them. But for the most part, people will not choose self-destructive behavior."

I paused. "Next question?"

A lady in her late thirties with long, curly red hair, asked incredulously, "Let me understand this correctly. You're saying that free love is going to be the norm in the near future? Everyone is going to be screwing each other?"

The audience laughed.

I smiled as the audience perked up at this sexual discussion. "To a certain extent, yes, that is true. More people

Chapter Seven - Seattle Lecture

will be open to sexuality as the taboo is lifted. However, monogamous relationships will still be the norm. People will prefer to pick partners and not use one-night stands for their sexual relationships.

"Understand, the next civilization will be much more spiritually aware. Life is going to be more unconditional. Thus, having a short-term relationship will be easier in the future. Today, it becomes very emotional and messy for short-term relationships to dissolve, and this creates a degree of fear from starting a relationship. This fear will largely go away, thereby making it much easier to form short-term relationships.

"Most people will have long-term faithful partners. Others will have a series of short relationships. Another change in the future is that currently, many couples do not allow friendships with the opposite sex. In the future, most people will realize that this is too restricting. People will know that they are God. There won't be the taboos that exist today. There won't be jealousy or fear…"

"No jealousy?" interrupted the lady. "Come on! You have to be kidding."

I paused, smiling and speaking slowly. "Our current beliefs will be transformed. Jealousy is an emotion created out of fear. I can tell you confidently that fear will be no more. It will disappear. And, with it, a whole host of emotions, such as anger, hostility, animosity, even jealousy. Yes, I am standing up here today, telling you that there will be no more jealousy. And the short-term relationships that you fear today will be welcomed in the future."

I paused to allow her to reply, but she looked back at me skeptically without speaking.

"Fun in the future will come from relationships. We will shun entertainment and sports in order to focus on each other. We will share our divinity. I know that this sounds incredible, and even boring. Even I have trouble believing it sometimes.

"We will decide, as survivors of this era, not to have competitive enterprises, because competitiveness breeds conflict. We will decide to exclude these kinds of experiences. As you can see, very few experiences will survive from our current civilization. The future will be nothing like life today.

"A world without competition doesn't seem possible, does it? But then, neither does a world based on love, a world in which peace and harmony will be a way of life. I submit that a world based on love will be much different from what we currently experience."

I bowed. "Thank you for coming. You can buy a book or order a digital recording of the lecture on your way out. If anyone has a book for me to sign, I will be up here for a while longer."

The crowd applauded, then rose and made their way to the exit. Several people approached the stage to ask us questions. Peter and I stayed for another twenty minutes, talking to people and signing books.

After we finished and walked outside, I looked at Peter with a warm smile. "We did it, and I think we did a good job. Do you want to join me again sometime?"

Peter paused in contemplation. "Sure. I would like to do it again but not for a while. I need to go back to the reservation and do some work."

I smiled. "Okay, we'll plan something in a few months. How about a lecture in Arizona?"

"Sure, Sedona would be good," he replied.

"Let's do two. One in Sedona and another in Tucson. That way we can visit Marilyn. I haven't seen her in a while."

Peter smiled. "Sure, I like meeting your friends."

Chapter Seven - Seattle Lecture

As Peter and I walked toward our hotel rooms, I felt more exhilarated than I ever had. This was as good as it gets, I thought. My life was as I wanted it, unfolding exactly the way I would have planned it. I wondered if I had.

Endnotes

1. *Messages from Michael*, Chelsea Quinn Yarbro, Berkeley Books, 1980.

2. *Spiritual Bill of Rights*, by St. Germain, Channeled through Isaac George, January 4th, 2002.

3. *Think on These Things*, J. Krishnamurti, HarperPerennial, 1964.

Chapter Seven - Seattle Lecture

www.ingramcontent.com/pod-product-compliance
Lightning Source LLC
Chambersburg PA
CBHW071925290426
44110CB00013B/1477